Much Ado About
MORMONS

Cover images: William F. Cody (Buffalo Bill), Courtesy of Library of Congress Prints and Photographic Division, Washington, DC. President Abraham Lincoln, Courtesy of Wikimedia commons; for more information, visit www.commons.wikimedia.org. Mark Twain, Courtesy of Wikimedia commons; for more information, visit www.commons.wikimedia.org. Mike Wallace, Courtesy of Deseret News. Sharon Osbourne, Sharon Osbourne © Neal Preston/CORBIS, ca. 2002. Sir Arthur Conan Doyle, Courtesy of Library of Congress Prints and Photographic Division, Washington, DC. President Lyndon B. Johnson, LBJ Library Photo by: Yoichi R. Okamoto, January 1969. Courtesy of Wikimedia commons; for more information, visit www.commons. Susan B. Anthony, Courtesy of Wikimedia commons; for more information, visit www.commons.wikimedia.org. President Franklin D. Roosevelt, Courtesy of Wikimedia commons; for more information, visit www.commons.wikimedia.org. President Jimmy Carter, Courtesy of Wikimedia commons; for more information, visit www.commons.wikimedia.org. Ralph Waldo Emerson, Courtesy of Wikimedia commons; for more information, visit www.commons.wikimedia.org. Angela Lansbury, courtesy of Deseret News.

Cover design copyright © 2011 by Covenant Communications, Inc.

Published by Covenant Communications, Inc.
American Fork, Utah

Copyright © 2011 by Rick Walton

All rights reserved. No part of this book may be reproduced in any format or in any medium without the written permission of the publisher, Covenant Communications, Inc., P.O. Box 416, American Fork, UT 84003. This work is not an official publication of The Church of Jesus Christ of Latter-day Saints. The views expressed within this work are the sole responsibility of the author and do not necessarily reflect the position of The Church of Jesus Christ of Latter-day Saints, Covenant Communications, Inc., or any other entity.

Printed in the United States of America
First Printing: April 2011

17 16 15 14 13 12 11 10 9 8 7 6 5 4 3 2 1

ISBN 978-1-60861-076-1

Much Ado About Mormons

Edited by Rick Walton

Covenant Communications, Inc.

TABLE OF CONTENTS

Charles Francis Adams and John Quincy—1844 1
John Greenleaf Whittier—1845 5
President James K. Polk—1846 15
William F. Cody (Buffalo Bill)—1857 19
Horace Greeley—1859 27
Sir Richard F. Burton—1860 33
Mark Twain—1861 45
President Abraham Lincoln—1863 51
Ralph Waldo Emerson—1863 53
Charles Dickens—1863 56
P. T. Barnum—1868 73
Susan B. Anthony—1871 77
Elizabeth Kane—1872 81
General George A. Custer—1875 95
Miriam Florence Leslie—1877 97
John Muir—1877 109
Lady Mary Duffus Hardy—1880 115
Sir Arthur Conan Doyle—1887 123
President Benjamin Harrison—1891 129
President Theodore Roosevelt—1911 131
Willa Cather—1918 135
President Warren G. Harding—1923 139
Sir Arthur Conan Doyle (Second Entry)—1923 141
President Franklin D. Roosevelt—1944 149
President Harry S Truman—1948 151
Cecil B. DeMille—1957 155
Harry Golden—1959 163

Vincent Price—1959	167
President Herbert Hoover—1960	169
President John F. Kennedy—1960–1963	173
Norman Vincent Peale—1963	179
President Lyndon B. Johnson—1964	181
Maria von Trapp—1965	183
Paul Harvey—1967	185
President Richard M. Nixon—1970	187
President Gerald R. Ford—1974–1978	191
Alvin Toffler—1980	195
Saul Bellow—1994	199
Margaret Thatcher—1996	203
President Jimmy Carter—2004	205
Mike Wallace—2005	209
Sharon Osbourne—2005	211
Ma Ying-jeou—2008	213
Mormon Tabernacle Choir Guests	215
Brian Stokes Mitchell—2008	217
Edward Herrmann—2008	219
Angela Lansbury—2001	223
Walter Cronkite—2002	225
Sissel Kyrkjebo—2006	227

Charles Francis Adams and John Quincy

In 1844, Charles Francis Adams, the son of President John Quincy Adams, and Charles's cousin Josiah Quincy, the mayor of Boston, traveled to Nauvoo. They recorded their impressions of the Prophet Joseph Smith, the Nauvoo Temple, and the Missouri persecutions the Saints suffered.

Josiah Quincy wrote,

> As Dr. Goforth introduced us to the prophet, he mentioned the parentage of my companion. "God bless you, to begin with!" said Joseph Smith, raising his hands in the air and letting them descend upon the shoulders of Mr. Adams. The benediction, though evidently sincere, had an odd savor of what may be called official familiarity, such as a crowned head might adopt on receiving the heir presumptive of a friendly court.
>
> Adams . . . wrote that they "were introduced to the celebrated Joe Smith. A middle-aged man with a shrewd but rather ordinary expression of countenance, unshaved and in clothes neither very choice nor neat."

Adams describes seeing the half-built Nauvoo Temple: "The architecture is original—and curious. It is built by the contribution of one-tenth of labor and goods. The prophet seems to have drawn his ideas largely from the Jewish system." Adams also expressed his sympathies upon hearing of the way the Mormons were driven from Missouri: "This is one of the most disgraceful chapters in the history of the United States, and shows that the spirit of intolerance, religious and political, can find a shelter even in the fairest professions of liberty." (Michael K. Winder, *Presidents and Prophets,* 37–38)

The Free Soil Banner—Martin Van Buren for president & Charles F. Adams for vice president in 1848

John Greenleaf Whittier

1845

The Prophet Joseph Smith had been dead only a year. The elders of the Church, their fervor, intensity, and sincerity swelled by the martyrdom, were holding meetings and preaching wherever they could. Into one such meeting in Lowell, Massachusetts, walked John Greenleaf Whittier. Mostly well known for his ballads, the famous Quaker poet was also a fiery abolitionist and politician who helped found the Republican Party.

A MORMON CONVENTICLE

Passing up Merrimack street the other day, my attention was arrested by a loud, earnest voice, apparently engaged in preaching, or rather "holding forth," in the second story of the building opposite. I was in the mood to welcome anything of a novel character; and following the sound, I passed up a flight of steps, leading to a long, narrow and somewhat shabby room, dignified by the appellation of Classic Hall.

Seating myself, I looked about me. There were from fifty to one hundred persons in the audience, in which nearly all classes of this heterogeneous community seemed pretty fairly represented, all listening with more or less attention to the speaker.

He was a young man, with dark, enthusiast complexion, black eyes and hair; with his collar thrown back, and his coat cuffs turned over, revealing a somewhat undue quantity of "fine linen," bending over his coarse board pulpit, and gesticulating with the vehemence of Hamlet's player, "tearing his passion to rags." A band of mourning crape, fluttering with the spasmodic action of his left arm, and an allusion to "our late beloved brother, Joseph Smith," sufficiently indicated the sect of the speaker. He was a Mormon—a Saint of the Latter Days!

His theme was the power of Faith. Although evidently unlearned, and innocent enough of dealing in such "abominable matters as a verb or a noun, which no Christian ear can endure," to have satisfied Jack Cade himself, there was a straitforward vehemence and intense earnestness in his manner, which at once disarmed my criticism. He spoke of Adam, in Paradise, as the lord of this lower world—"For," said he, "water could n't drown him, fire could n't burn him, cold could n't freeze him—nothing could harm him, for he had all the elements under his feet. And what, my hearers, was the secret of this power? His faith in God! That was it. Well, the Devil wanted this power. He behaved in a mean, *ungentlemanly* way, and deceived Eve, and lied to her, he did. And so Adam lost his faith. And all this power over the elements that Adam had, the Devil got, and has it now. He is the Prince and Power of the air, *consequently* he is master of the elements, and lord of this world. He has filled it with unbelief, and robbed man of his birthright, and will do so, until the hour of the Power of Darkness is ended, and the mighty angel comes down with the chain in his hand to bind the Old Serpent and Dragon." He dwelt with great earnestness on the power of Faith, and cited examples from the Scriptures. It was by a perfect faith in God, that Enoch was enabled to "walk with Him," and overcome death itself, and have dominion over the elements, so that, "instead of dying, *God suspended the laws of gravitation,* and took him right up bodily." Finally it was by Faith that the doctrines of the Latter Day Saints were preached, and marvellous things wrought, and the estate of Adam in Paradise once more attained.

John Greenleaf Whittier enjoying the afternoon with friends

Another speaker, a stout, black-browed "son of thunder," gave an interesting account of his experience. He had been one of the apostles of the Mormon Evangel, and had visited Europe. He went in faith. He had "but three cents in his pocket" when he reached England. He went to the high professors of all sects, and they would not receive him; they pronounced him "damned already." He was reduced to great poverty and hunger: alone in a strange land, with no one to bid him welcome. He was on the very verge of starvation. "Then," said he, "I knelt down, and I prayed in earnest faith, 'Lord, give me this day my daily bread!' O, I tell ye, *I prayed with a good appetite*; and I rose up, and was moved to go to a house near at hand. I knocked at the door, and when the owner came, I said to him, 'I am a minister of the Lord Jesus Christ from America. I am starving—will you give me some food?' 'Why, bless you! yes!' said the man, 'sit down and eat as much as you please.' And I *did* sit down at his table, blessed be God! But, my hearers, he was not a professor; he was not a Christian, but one of Robert Owen's infidels. The Lord reward him for his kindness!"

In listening to these modern prophets, I discovered, as I think, the great secret of their

> *I knelt down, and I prayed in earnest faith, "Lord, give me this day my daily bread!"*

success in making converts. They speak to a common feeling; they minister to a universal want. They contrast strongly the miraculous power of the gospel in the apostolic time with the present state of our nominal Christianity. They ask for the signs of divine power; the faith overcoming all things, which opened the prison doors of the apostles, gave them power over the elements, which rebuked disease and death itself, and made visible to all the presence of the Living God. They ask for any declaration in the Scriptures that this miraculous power of faith was to be confined to the first confessors of Christianity. They speak a language of hope and promise to weak, weary hearts, tossed and troubled, who have wandered from sect to sect, seeking in vain for the primal manifestations of the Divine power. They tell them, that in these latter days Faith is again in the world; that the universe is not a blind, dark mechanism; but that God's Spirit moves in it yet; that something of the same power which sealed the jaws of lions, made harmless the furnace of Babylon—which enabled Peter to heal the sick, and Paul to shake off unharmed the viper of Malta, is yet vouchsafed to the saints of Nauvoo. Men who have struggled with unbelief and dark thoughts; who long for some tangible, visible evidence of Christianity, literally hungering and thirsting after a miracle, grasp at the Mormon delusion, as the long desired manifestation—"the sought Kalon found."

In speaking of Mormonism as a delusion, I refer more particularly to the apochryphal Book of Mormon. That the great majority of the "Latter Day Saints" are honest and sincere fanatics, I have no reason to doubt. They have made great sacrifices, and endured severe and protracted persecution for their faith. The reports circulated against them by their unprincipled enemies in the West, are in the main destitute of foundation. I place no dependence upon charges made against them by the ruffian mob of the Mississippi valley, and the reckless slave-drivers, who, at the point of the bayonet and bowie knife, expelled them from Missouri, and signalized their Christian crusade against unbelievers by murdering old men, and violating their innocent wives and daughters. It is natural that the wrong-doers should hate those whom they have so foully injured.

A replica of Robert Fulton's Clermont, *America's first steamboat, in 1907*

The Prophet himself, the Master Spirit of this extraordinary religious movement, is no more. He died by the hands of wicked and barbarous men, a martyr, unwilling, doubtless, but still a martyr, of his Faith. For, after all, Joe Smith could not have been wholly insincere. Or, if so in the outset, it is more than probable that his extraordinary success, his wonderful power over the minds of men, caused him to seem a miracle and a marvel to himself, and, like Mohammed and Napoleon, to consider himself a chosen instrument of the Eternal Power.

In the "Narrative of an eye witness of the Mormon Massacre," published in a Western paper, I was a good deal impressed by the writer's account of the departure of the Prophet from "the holy city," to deliver himself up to the state authorities at Warsaw. It was well understood, that in so doing, he was about to subject himself to extreme hazard. The whole country round about was swarming with armed men, eager to embrue their hands in his blood. The city was in a fearful state of alarm and excitement. The great Nauvoo legion, with its two thousand strong of armed fanatics, was drawn up in the principal square. A word from the Prophet would have converted that dark, silent mass into desperate and unsparing defenders of their leader and the holy places of their faith. Mounted on his favorite black horse, he rode through the glittering files; and with words of cheer and encouragement, exhorted them to obey the laws of the state, and give their enemies no excuse for persecution and outrage. "Well!" said he, as he left them, "they are good boys, if I never see them again." Taking leave of his family, and his more intimate friends, he turned his horse, and rode up in front of the great temple, as if to take a final look at the proudest trophy of his power. After contemplating it for awhile in silence, he put spurs to his horse, in company with his brother, who, it will be recollected, shared his fate in the prison, dashed away towards Warsaw, and the prairie horizon shut down between him and the City of the Saints for the last time.

Once in the world's history we were to have a Yankee prophet, and we have had him in Joe Smith. For good or for evil, he has left his track on the great pathway of life—or, to use the words of Horne, "knocked out for himself a window in the wall of the nineteenth century," whence his rude, bold, good-humored face will peer out upon the generations to come. But, the Prophet has not trusted his fame merely to the keeping of the spiritual. He has incorporated himself with the enduring stone of the great Nauvoo temple, which, when completed, will be the most splendid and imposing architectural monument in the New World. With its huge walls of hewn stone—its thirty gigantic pillars, loftier than those of Baalbec—their massive caps carved into the likeness of enormous human faces, themselves resting upon crescent moons, with a giant profile of a face within the curve,—it stands upon the

A temple unique and wonderful as the faith of its builder

highest elevation of the most beautiful city-site of the West, overlooking the "Father of Waters;"—a temple unique and wonderful as the faith of its builder, embodying in its singular and mysterious architecture, the Titan idea of the Pyramids, and the solemn and awe-inspiring thought which speaks from the Gothic piles of the middle ages. The conception of such a work gives dignity and beauty even to the coarse and vulgar character of the Mormon Prophet, and almost leads us to credit his claim of inspiration:

The hand that rounded Peter's dome,
And groined the aisles of Christian Rome,
Wrought in a sad sincerity;
Himself from God he could not free;
He builded better than he knew—
The conscious stone to beauty grew

(John Greenleaf Whittier, *The Stranger in Lowell*, 26–32)

President James K. Polk

President James K. Polk approached his presidency with four well-defined goals for the nation, the fourth being to acquire California. However, President Polk anticipated buying California—not having to fight for it. When the annexation of Texas soured Mexico's relationship with the United States, President Polk faced an unexpected obstacle to his goal, the Mexican War. He didn't want to also have to deal with a war with the Mormons, or between the Mormons and their neighbors, so when he was visited by Mormon representatives he was pleased to come up with a solution that helped both the Mormons and his country.

Held a conversation with Mr. Amos Kendall & Mr. J. C. Little of Petersborough, N. H. (a mormon) to-day. They desired to see me in relation to a large body of Mormon emigrants who are now on their way from Na[u]voo & other parts of the U.S. to California, and to learn the policy of the Government towards them. I told Mr. Little that by our constitution the mormons would be treated as all other American citizens were, without regard to the sect to which they belonged or the religious creed which they professed, and that I had no prejudices towards them which could induce a different course of treatment. Mr. Little said that they were Americans in all their feelings, & friends of the U.S. I told Mr. Little that we were at war with Mexico, and asked him if 500 or more of the mormons now on their way to California would be willing on their arrival in that country to volunteer and enter the U.S. army in that war, under the command of a U.S. officer. He said he had no doubt they would willingly do so.* He said if the U.S. would receive them into the service he would immediately proceed and overtake the emigrants now on the way and make the arrangement with them to do so. . . . It was with the view to prevent this singular sect from becoming hostile to the U.S. that I held the conference with Mr. Little, and with the same view I am to see him again to-morrow. (James Knox Polk, *The Diary of James K. Polk During His Presidency*, 1:445–46)

He had no doubt they would willingly do so.

---

* At first the Mormons were hesitant to participate in the Mormon Battalion, fearing that raising an army was another way the United States planned to persecute the Saints. Brigham Young, however, recognized that the government was trying to help the migrating Mormons by allowing them to prove their loyalty, earn money, and encamp on U.S. lands in return for providing an army. Eventually, 543 men enlisted and marched from Council Bluffs, Iowa, to San Diego, California. It was one of the longest marches in U.S. military history. The Mormons never had to fight any Mexican soldiers, but they faced rugged conditions, hot temperatures, food scarcity, illness, and a run-in with a herd of wild cattle. After arriving in California, some soldiers marched back to Fort Leavenworth in Kansas and others stayed to serve garrison duty. The Mormon Battalion is remembered for contributing to the growth of California by building homes, a courthouse, and a fort. After being discharged from the military, some Mormon Battalion members were among the first to find gold in California.

The Mormon Battalion in an 1846 painting by George M. Ottinger

William F. Cody (Buffalo Bill)

1857

Buffalo Bill was a frontiersman, an army scout, a buffalo hunter, and a showman who traveled throughout the world performing "Buffalo Bill's Wild West Show." He seems to have enjoyed the role of storyteller, too—claiming falsely to have ridden for the Pony Express and writing an exaggerated autobiography. Dime novels were written about him, and stories are still told about his adventures. One adventure Buffalo Bill wrote about was when he rode with Johnston's army as a scout on the way to subdue the rebellious Mormons. The army needed an enormous amount of supplies, but they didn't get much of what they needed, thanks to the Mormon "guerrillas" who snuck up on army supply trains, scattered their livestock, and destroyed their wagons. Following is Buffalo Bill's story. The "Joe" Smith mentioned is most likely "Lot" Smith, an easy enough mistake to make if you don't know your Mormon history and you're not a stickler for facts.

CAPTURED BY DANITES*

The next day we rolled out of camp and proceeded on our way towards the setting sun. Everything ran along smoothly with us from that point until we came within about eighteen miles of Green River, in the Rocky Mountains—where we camped at noon. At this place we had to drive our cattle about a mile and a half to a creek to water them. Simpson, his assistant George Woods and myself, accompanied by the usual number of guards, drove the cattle over to the creek, and while on our way back to camp we suddenly observed a party of twenty horsemen rapidly approaching us. We were not yet in view of our wagons, as a rise of ground intervened, and therefore we could not signal the train-men in case of any unexpected danger befalling us. We had no suspicion, however, that we were about to be trapped, as the strangers were white men. When they had come up to us, one of the party, who evidently was the leader, rode out in front and said:—

"How are you, Mr. Simpson?"

"You've got the best of me, sir," said Simpson, who did not know him.

"Well, I rather think I have," coolly replied the stranger, whose words conveyed a double meaning, as we soon learned. We had all come to a halt by this time and the strange horsemen had surrounded us. They were all armed with double-barreled shot guns, rifles and revolvers. We also were armed with revolvers, but we had had no idea of danger, and these men, much to our surprise, had "got the drop" on us and had covered us with their weapons, so that we were completely at their mercy. The whole movement of corraling us was done so quietly and quickly that it was accomplished before we knew it.

"I'll trouble you for your six shooters, gentlemen," now said the leader.

"I'll give 'em to you in a way you don't want,"

replied Simpson.

The next moment three guns were leveled at Simpson. "If you make a move you're a dead man," said the leader.

Simpson saw that he was taken at a great disadvantage, and thinking it advisable not to risk the lives of the party by any rash act on his part, he said: "I see now that you have the best of me, but who are you, anyhow?"

"I am Joe Smith," was the reply.

"What! the leader of the Danites?" asked Simpson.

If you make a move you're a dead man.

"You are correct," said Smith, for he it was.

"Yes," said Simpson, "I know you now; you are a spying scoundrel."

Simpson had good reason for calling him this and applying to him a much more opprobrious epithet, for only a short time before this, Joe Smith had visited our train in the disguise of a teamster, and had remained with us two days. He suddenly disappeared, no one knowing where he had gone or why he had come among us. But it was all explained to us now that he had returned with his Mormon Danites. After they had disarmed us, Simpson asked, "Well, Smith, what are you going to do with us?"

"Ride back with us and I'll soon show you," said Smith.

DESTRUCTION OF THE TRAIN BY MORMONS

We had no idea of the surprise which awaited us. As we came upon the top of the ridge, from which we could view our camp, we were astonished to see the remainder of the train-men disarmed and stationed in a group and surrounded by another squad of Danites, while other Mormons were searching our wagons for such articles as they wanted.

"How is this?" inquired Simpson. "How did you surprise my camp without a struggle? I can't understand it."

"Easily enough," said Smith; "your men were all asleep under the wagons, except the cooks,

William F. Cody and an Indian troop member from his Wild West Show in 1907

who saw us coming and took us for returning Californians or emigrants, and paid no attention to us until we rode up and surrounded your train. With our arms covering the men, we woke them up, and told them all they had to do was to walk out and drop their pistols—which they saw was the best thing they could do under circumstances over which they had no control—and you can just bet they did it."

"And what do you propose to do with us now?" asked Simpson.

"I intend to burn your train," said he; "you are loaded with supplies and ammunition for Sidney Johnston, and as I have no way to convey the stuff to my own people, I'll see that it does not reach the United States troops."

"Are you going to turn us adrift here?" asked Simpson, who was anxious to learn what was to become of himself and his men.

"No; I am hardly so bad as that. I'll give you enough provisions to last you until you can reach Fort Bridger," replied Smith; "and as soon as your cooks can get the stuff out of the wagons, you can start."

"On foot?" was the laconic inquiry of Simpson.

"Yes, sir," was the equally short reply.

"Smith, that's too rough on us men. Put yourself in our place and see how you would like it," said Simpson; "you can well afford to give us at least one wagon and six yokes of oxen to convey us and our clothing and provisions to Fort Bridger. You're a brute if you don't do this."

"Well," said Smith, after consulting a minute or two with some of his company, "I'll do that much for you."

The cattle and the wagon were brought up according to his orders, and the clothing and provisions were loaded on.

"Now you can go," said Smith, after everything had been arranged.

"Joe Smith, I think you are a mean coward to set us afloat in a hostile country without giving us our arms," said Simpson, who had once before asked for the weapons, and had had his request denied.

Smith, after further consultation with his comrades, said: "Simpson, you are too brave a man to be turned adrift here without any means of defense. You shall have your revolvers and guns." Our weapons were accordingly handed over to Simpson, and we at once started for Fort Bridger, knowing that it would be useless to attempt the recapture of our train.

When we had traveled about two miles we saw the smoke arising from our old camp. The Mormons after taking what goods they wanted and could carry off, had set fire to the wagons, many of which were loaded with bacon, lard, hardtack, and other provisions, which made a very hot, fierce fire, and the smoke to roll up in dense clouds. Some of the wagons were loaded with ammunition, and it was not long before loud explosions followed in rapid succession. We waited and witnessed the burning of the train, and then pushed on to Fort Bridger. Arriving at this post, we learned that two other trains had been captured and destroyed in the same way, by the Mormons. This made seventy-five wagon loads, or 450,000 pounds of supplies, mostly provisions, which never reached General Johnston's command to which they had been consigned. (Buffalo Bill, *Life and Adventures of "Buffalo Bill,"* 50–53.)

*The Danites were a secret military organized during the Missouri period of Church history to provide defense and retaliation against those who terrorized Mormons. The organizer of the group, Sampson Avard, was later arrested and went free by falsely accusing the First Presidency of commanding his illegal actions. This group of Danites is not to be confused with those later appointed by Brigham Young in Utah to act as a police force when there were no civil authorities. These "Danites" were frontiersmen who dealt with rough characters passing through the state (Saints who committed crimes were disciplined by their ecclesiastical leaders). The term "Danites" was applied to Brigham Young's lawmen by the Eastern press, although it's not clear if any of them were ever members of Sampson Avard's original group. These men were roughriders who served in the Utah War and defended the Saints against attacks from outsiders, but it seems their violent and sometimes illegal activities were greatly exaggerated by anti-Mormon publications. By 1869, they were all retired or had died, and civil authorities had taken over policing the territory.

Colonel William F. Cody "Buffalo Bill"—an American showman—in 1907

HORACE GREELEY

Horace Greeley, the founder and editor of the New York Tribune, *was one of the most influential journalists of his time. He was a social reformer, he dabbled in politics, and he challenged President Lincoln to free the slaves. His bold editorial served as a precursor to Lincoln's Emancipation Proclamation. Greeley is often attributed for the quote, "Go West, young man, and grow up with the country." He decided to see for himself how the country was growing up when he traveled west himself. In July 1859, he spent ten days among the Mormons and recorded what he saw through his journalist eyes.*

THE MORMONS AND MORMONISM

I had been told that the Mormons were remarkably ignorant, superstitious, and brutalized; but the aspect of these congregations did not sustain that assertion. Very few rural congregations would exhibit more heads evincing decided ability; and I doubt whether any assemblage, so largely European in its composition, would make a better appearance. Not that Europeans are less intellectual or comely than Americans; but our emigrants are mainly of the poorer classes; and poverty, privation, and rugged toil, plow hard, forbidding lines in the human countenance elsewhere than in Utah. Brigham Young was not present at either service.

Do I regard the great body of these Mormons as knaves and hypocrites? Assuredly not. I do not believe there was ever a religion whereof the great mass of the adherents were not honest and sincere. Hypocrites and knaves there are in all sects; it is quite possible that some of the magnates of the Mormon Church regard this so-called religion (with all others) as a contrivance for the enslavement and fleecing of the many, and the aggrandizement of the few; but I cannot believe that a sect, so considerable and so vigorous as the Mormon, was ever founded in conscious imposture, or built up on any other basis than that of earnest conviction. . . .

Nor do I accept the current Gentile presumption, that the Mormons are an organized banditti—a horde of robbers and assassins. Thieves and murderers mainly haunt the purlieus of great cities, or hide in caverns and forests adjacent to the great routes of travel. But when the Mormon leaders decided to set up their Zion in these parched mountain vales and cañons, the said valleys were utterly secluded and remote from all Gentile approach—away from any mail-route or channel

> *I do not believe there was ever a religion whereof the great mass of the adherents were not honest and sincere.*

of emigration. That the Mormons wished to escape Gentile control, scrutiny, jurisprudence, is evident; that they meant to abuse their inaccessibility, to the detriment and plunder of wayfarers, is not credible. (Horace Greeley, *An Overland Journey*, 222–24)

The church is rich, and is hourly increasing in wealth; the church settles all civil controversies which elsewhere cause lawsuits; the church spends little or nothing, yet rules everything; while the federal government, though spending two or three millions per annum here, and keeping up a fussy

Horace Greeley and family at home, a painting done by Otto Knirsch

Horace Greeley in 1871, a print by Johnson & Fry after a painting by Chappel

parade of authority, is powerless and despised. If, then, we are to have "popular sovereignty" in the territories, let us have it pure and without shams. Let Brigham be reappointed governor; withdraw the present federal office-holders and army; open shorter and better roads to California through the country north of Bridger; and notify the emigrants that, if they choose to pass through Utah, they will do so at their own risk. Let the Mormons have the territory to themselves—it is worth very little to others, but reduce its area by cutting off Carson Valley on the one side, and making a Rocky Mountain territory on the other, and then let them go on their way rejoicing. I believe this is not only by far the cheapest but the safest and best mode of dealing with the difficulties already developed and daily developing here, unless the notion of "popular sovereignty" in the territories is to be utterly exploded and given up. "Popular Sovereignty" in a territory is a contradiction of terms; but "popular sovereignty" in a territory backed by a thousand sharp federal bayonets and a battery of flying artillery, is too monstrous a futility, too transparent a swindle, to be much longer upheld or tolerated. (228–29)

> *Let the Mormons have the territory . . . and then let them go on their way rejoicing.*

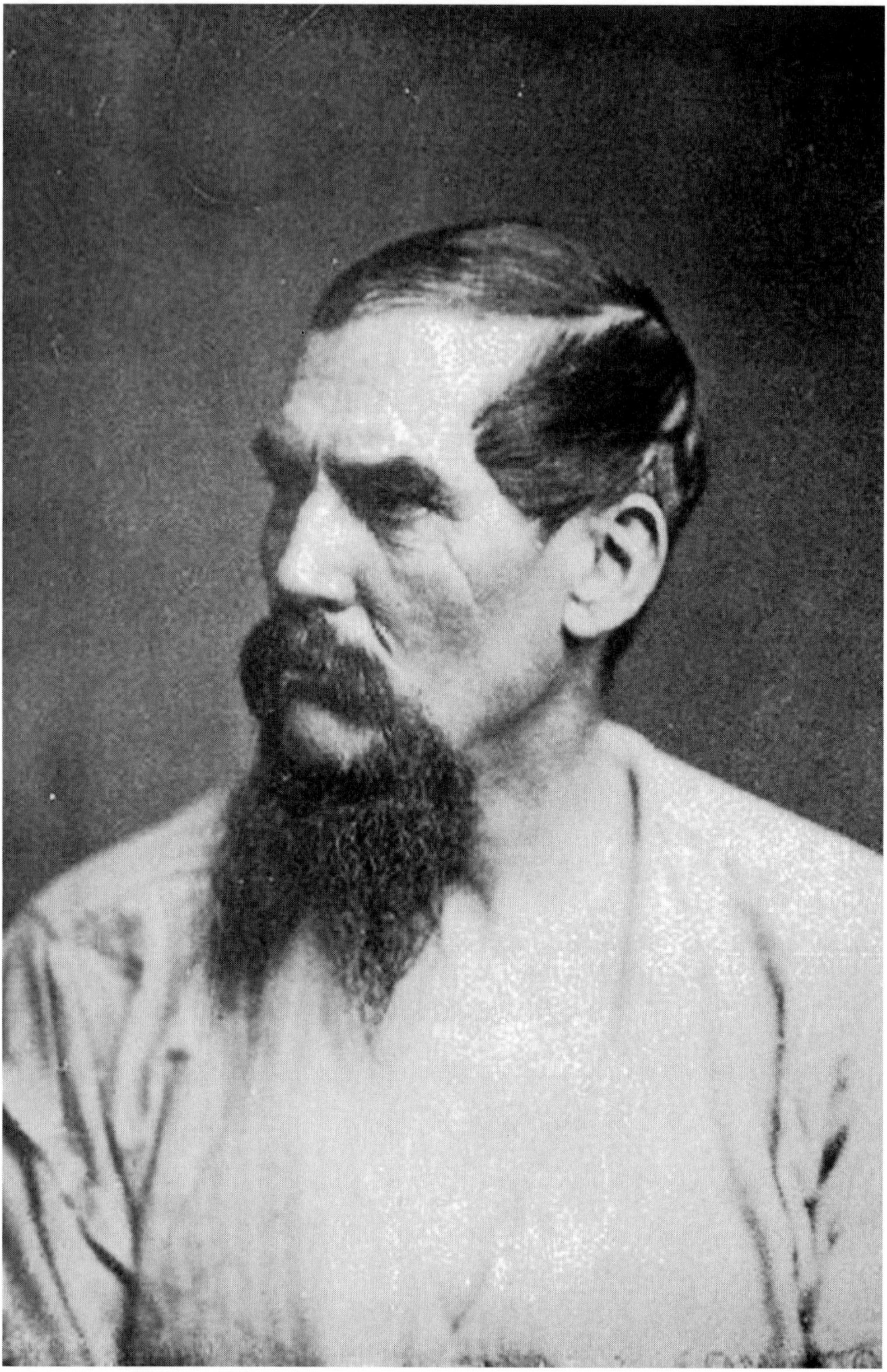

Sir Richard F. Burton

1860

Sir Richard F. Burton was born in England but explored the world. He worked for the East India Company, where he learned Middle Eastern languages and became familiar with their cultures. Sometimes he traveled in disguise, such as when he made the pilgrimage to Mecca like Middle Eastern natives. Later he traveled to Africa and Brazil. An explorer, scholar, soldier, translator of The Arabian Nights *and dozens of other books, the man Disney can thank for having introduced Aladdin to the western world and an expert on polygamous cultures, he visited the "City of the Saints" from August 25 to September 20, 1860. The result: a huge volume written by a remarkable man about a remarkable people.*

VISIT TO THE PROPHET

Shortly after arriving, I had mentioned to Governor Cumming my desire to call upon Mr., or rather, as his official title is, President, Brigham Young, and he honoured me by inquiring what time would be most convenient to him. The following was the answer . . .

"Governor A. Cumming.

"Great Salt Lake City, Aug. 30, 1860.

"Sir,—In reply to your note of the 29th inst., I embrace the earliest opportunity since my return, to inform you that it will be agreeable to me to meet the gentleman you mention in my office at 11 A.M. tomorrow, the 31st.

Brigham Young"

The "President of the Church of Jesus Christ of Latter-Day Saints all over the World" is obliged to use caution in admitting strangers, not only for personal safety, but also to defend his dignity from the rude and unfeeling remarks of visitors, who seem to think themselves entitled, in the case of a Mormon, to transgress every rule of civility.

About noon, after a preliminary visit to Mr. Gilbert—and a visit in these lands always entails a certain amount of "smiling"—I met Governor Cumming in Main Street, and we proceeded together to our visit. After a slight scrutiny we passed the guard—which is dressed in plain clothes and to the eye unarmed—and walking down the verandah, entered the Prophet's private office. Several people who were sitting there rose at Mr. Cumming's entrance. At a few words of introduction, Mr. Brigham Young advanced, shook hands with complete simplicity of manner, asked me to be seated on a sofa at one side of the room, and presented me to those present.

Under ordinary circumstances it would be unfair in a visitor to draw the portrait of one visited. But this is no common case. I have violated no rites of hospitality. Mr. Brigham Young is a "seer, revelator, and prophet, having all the gifts of God which He bestows upon the Head of the Church:" his memoirs, lithographs, photographs, and portraits have been published again and again; I add but one more likeness; and, finally, I have nothing to say except in his favour.

The Prophet was born at Whittingham, Vermont, on the 1st of June, 1801; he was consequently, in 1860, fifty-nine years of age: he looks about forty-five. *La célébrité vieillit*—I had expected to see a venerable-looking old man. Scarcely a grey thread appears in his hair, which is parted on the side, light colored, rather thick, and reaches below the ears with a half curl. He formerly wore it long, after the Western style; now it is cut level with the ear-lobes. The forehead is somewhat narrow, the eyebrows are thin, the eyes between grey and blue, with a calm, composed, and

President Brigham Young of The Church of Jesus Christ of Latter-day Saints, circa 1860s

somewhat reserved expression: a slight droop in the left lid made me think that he had suffered from paralysis, I afterwards heard that the ptosis is the result of a neuralgia which has long tormented him. For this reason he usually covers his head—except in his own house or in the tabernacle. Mrs. Ward, who is followed by the "Revue des Deux-Mondes," therefore errs again in asserting that "his Mormon majesty never removes his hat in public." The nose, which is fine and somewhat sharp pointed, is bent a little to the left. The lips are close like the New Englander's, and the teeth, especially those of the under jaw, are imperfect. The cheeks are rather fleshy, and the line between the alæ of the nose and the mouth is broken; the chin is somewhat peaked, and the face clean shaven, except under the jaws, where the beard is allowed to grow. The hands are well made, and not disfigured by rings. The figure is somewhat large, broad-shouldered, and stooping a little when standing.

The Prophet's dress was neat and plain as a Quaker's, all grey homespun, except the cravat and waistcoat. His coat was of antique cut, and, like the pantaloons, baggy, and the buttons were black. A neck-tie of dark silk, with a large bow, was loosely passed round a starchless collar, which turned down of its own accord. The waistcoat was of black satin—once an article of almost national dress—single-breasted, and buttoned nearly to the neck, and a plain gold chain was passed into the pocket. The boots were Wellingtons, apparently of American make.

Altogether the Prophet's appearance was that of a gentleman farmer in New England—in fact, such as he is: his father was an agriculturist and revolutionary soldier, who settled "down East." He is a well-preserved man; a fact which some attribute to his habit of sleeping, as the Citizen Proudhon so strongly advises, in solitude. His manner is at once affable and impressive, simple and courteous: his want of pretension contrasts favorably with certain pseudo-prophets that I have seen, each and every of whom holds himself to be a "Logos" without other claim save a semi-maniacal self-esteem. He shows no signs of dogmatism, bigotry, or fanaticism, and never once entered—with me at least—upon the subject of religion. He impresses a stranger with a certain sense of power: his followers are, of course, wholly fascinated by his superior strength of brain. It is commonly said there is only one chief in Great Salt Lake City, and that is "Brigham." His temper is even and placid, his manner is cold—in fact, like his face, somewhat bloodless; but he is neither morose nor methodistic, and where occasion requires, he can use all the weapons of ridicule to direful effect, and "speak a bit of his mind" in a style which no one forgets. He often reproves his erring followers in purposely violent language, making the terrors of a scolding the punishment in lieu of hanging for a stolen horse or cow. His powers of observation are intuitively strong, and his friends declare him to be gifted with an excellent memory and a perfect judgment of character. If he dislikes a stranger at the first interview, he never sees him again. Of his temperance and sobriety there is but one opinion. His life is ascetic: his favorite food is baked potatoes with a little buttermilk, and his drink water: he disapproves, as do all strict Mormons, of spirituous liquors, and never touches anything stronger than a glass of thin Lager-bier; moreover, he abstains from tobacco. Mr. Hyde has accused him of habitual intemperance: he is, as his appearance shows, rather disposed to abstinence than to the reverse. Of his education I cannot speak: "men not books—deeds not words," has ever been his motto: he probably has, as Mr. Randolph said of Mr. Johnston, "a mind uncorrupted by books." In the only discourse which I heard him deliver, he pronounced impetus, impētus. Yet he converses with ease and correctness, has neither snuffle nor pompousness, and speaks as an authority upon certain subjects, such as agriculture and stock-breeding. He assumes no airs of extra sanctimoniousness, and has the plain, simple manners of honesty. His followers deem him an angel of light, his foes, a goblin damned: he is, I presume, neither one nor the other. I cannot pronounce about his scrupulousness: all the world over, the sincerest religious belief, and the practice of devotion, are sometimes compatible not only with the most disorderly life, but with the most terrible crimes; for mankind mostly believes that—

"Il est avec le ciel des accommodements."

He has been called hypocrite, swindler, forger, murderer. No one looks it less. The best authori-

The Mormon Battalion raising the flag, Los Angeles, California, July 4, 1847

ties—from those who accuse Mr. Joseph Smith of the heartless deception, to those who believe that he began as an impostor and ended as a prophet—find in Mr. Brigham Young "an earnest, obstinate egotistic enthusiasm, fanned by persecution and inflamed by bloodshed." He is the St. Paul of the New Dispensation: true and sincere, he gave point, and energy, and consistency to the somewhat disjointed, turbulent, and unforeseeing fanaticism of Mr. Joseph Smith; and if he has not been able to create, he has shown himself great in controlling circumstances. Finally, there is a total absence of pretension in his manner, and he has been so long used to power that he cares nothing for its display. The arts by which he rules the heterogeneous mass of conflicting elements are indomitable will, profound secrecy, and uncommon astuteness....

The Prophet received us in his private office, where he transacts the greater part of his business, corrects his sermons, and conducts his correspondence. It is a plain, neat room, with the usual conveniences, a large writing-desk and money-safe, table, sofas, and chairs, all made by

Sir Richard Burton, by Sir P. Leighton, National Portrait Gallery

the able mechanics of the settlement. I remarked a pistol and a rifle hung within ready reach on the right-hand wall; one of these is, I was told, a newly invented twelve-shooter. There was a look of order, which suited the character of the man: it is said that a door badly hinged, or a curtain hung awry, "puts his eye out." His style of doing business at the desk or in the field—for the Prophet does not disdain handiwork—is to issue distinct, copious, and intelligible directions to his *employés,* after which he dislikes referring to the subject. It is typical of his mode of acting, slow, deliberate, and conclusive. He has the reputation of being wealthy. He rose to power a poor man. The Gentiles naturally declare that he enriched himself by the tithes and plunder of his followers, and especially by preying upon and robbing the Gentiles. I believe, however, that no one pays church-dues and alms with more punctuality than the Prophet, and that he has far too many opportunities of coining money, safely and honestly, to be guilty, like some desperate destitute, of the short-sighted folly of fraud. In 1859 he owned, it is said, to being possessed of $250,000, equal to £50,000: which makes a millionaire in these mountains—it is too large a sum to jeopardize. . . .

After the few first words of greeting, I interpreted the Prophet's look to mean, that he would not dislike to know my object in the City of the Saints. I told him, that having read and heard much about Utah as it is said to be, I was anxious to see Utah as it is. He then entered briefly upon the subjects of stock and agriculture, and described the several varieties of soil. One delicate topic was touched upon: he alluded to the "Indian wars," as they are here called: he declared that when twenty are reported killed and wounded, that two or three would be nearer the truth, and that he could do more with a few pounds of flour and yards of cloth, than all the sabres of the camp could effect. The sentiment was cordially seconded by all present. . . .

The conversation, which lasted about an hour, ended by the Prophet asking me the line of my last African exploration, and whether it was the same country traversed by Dr. Livingstone. I replied, that it was about 10 degrees north of the Zambezi. Mr. A. Carrington rose to point out the place upon a map which hung against the wall, and placed his finger too near the equator, when Mr. Brigham Young said, "A little lower down." There are many educated men in England who could not have corrected the mistake as well. . . .

When conversation began to flag, we rose up, shook hands, as is the custom here, all round, and took leave. The first impression left upon my mind by this short séance, and it was subsequently confirmed, was, that the Prophet is no common man, and that he has none of the weakness and vanity which characterize the common uncommon man. A desultory conversation cannot be expected to draw out a master spirit, but a truly distinguished character exercises most often an instinctive—some would call it a mesmeric—effect upon those who come in contact with it; and as we hate or despise at first sight, and love or like at first sight, so Nature teaches us at first sight what to respect. It is observable that, although every Gentile writer has represented Mr. Joseph Smith as a heartless impostor, few have ventured to apply the term to Mr. Brigham Young. I also remarked an instance of the veneration shown by his followers, whose affection for him is equaled only by the confidence with which they entrust to him their dearest interests in this world and in the next. After my visit many congratulated me, as would the followers of the Tien Wong or heavenly King, upon having at last seen what they consider "a per se" the most remarkable man in the world. (Sir Richard Burton, *The City of the Saints,* 237–40, 242–45)

> *It was subsequently confirmed, was, that the Prophet is no common man.*

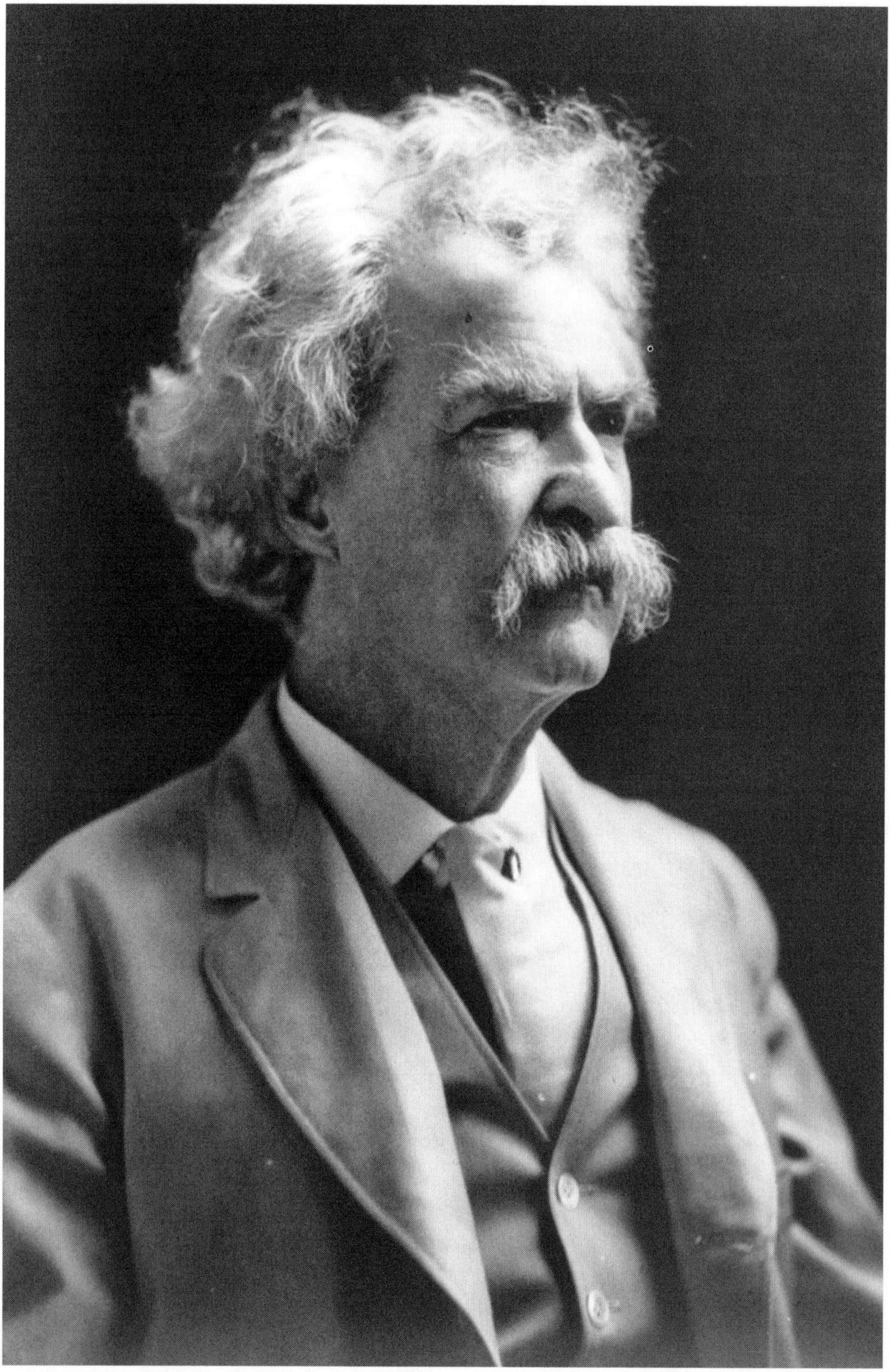

Mark Twain

1861

Twenty-six-year-old Samuel Clemens was on his way west with his brother Orion, who had just been appointed secretary of the Nevada territory, when he stayed just two days in Salt Lake City. But it was long enough for him to gather material for several chapters in his book, Roughing It, *a tome about living on the Western frontier. The book was published ten years later under the pseudonym Mark Twain, a term meaning "two fathoms deep," that he picked up while working as a river pilot on the Mississippi in 1857. The Civil War ended Twain's river career, and, after failing in other business ventures in Nevada, Twain eventually found success writing humorous newspaper articles and satirical books. He became a famous author and lecturer, and his masterpiece,* The Adventures of Huckleberry Finn, *is considered by some experts as the first realistic, modern American novel. The following narration picks up just after Twain and his party arrive in Salt Lake.*

We had a fine supper, of the freshest meats and fowls and vegetables—a great variety, and as great abundance. We walked about the streets some, afterward, and glanced in at shops and stores; and there was fascination in surreptitiously staring at every creature we took to be a Mormon. This was fairyland to us, to all intents and purposes—a land of enchantment, and goblins, and awful mystery. We felt a curiosity to ask every child how many mothers it had, and if it could tell them apart; and we experienced a thrill every time a dwelling-house door opened and shut as we passed, disclosing a glimpse of human heads and backs and shoulders—for we so longed to have a good satisfying look at a Mormon family in all its comprehensive ampleness, disposed in the customary concentric rings of its home circle. (Mark Twain, *Roughing It,* 93)

Next day we strolled about everywhere through the broad, straight, level streets, and enjoyed the pleasant strangeness of a city of fifteen thousand inhabitants with no loafers perceptible in it; and no visible drunkards or noisy people; a limpid stream rippling and dancing through every street in place of a filthy gutter; block after block of trim dwellings, built of "frame" and sunburned brick—a great thriving orchard and garden behind every one of them, apparently—branches from the street stream winding and sparkling among the garden-beds and fruit trees—and a grand general air of neatness, repair, thrift, and comfort, around and about and

> *A grand general air of neatness, repair, thrift, and comfort, around and about and over the whole.*

over the whole. And everywhere were workshops, factories, and all manner of industries; and intent faces and busy hands were to be seen wherever one looked; and in one's ears was the ceaseless clink of hammers, the buzz of trade and the contented hum of drums and fly-wheels. (94–95)

Salt Lake City was healthy—an extremely healthy city. They declared that there was only one physician in the place and he was arrested every week regularly and held to answer under the vagrant act for having "no visible means of support." (96)

Samuel Clemens—"Mark Twain"—a master of American literature

The second day, we made the acquaintance of Mr. Street (since deceased) and put on white shirts and went and paid a state visit to the king. He seemed a quiet, kindly, easy-mannered, dignified, self-possessed old gentleman of fifty-five or sixty, and had a gentle craft in his eye that probably belonged there. He was very simply dressed and was just taking off a straw hat as we entered. He talked about Utah, and the Indians, and Nevada, and general American matters and questions, with our secretary and certain government officials who came with us. But he never paid any attention to me, notwithstanding I made several attempts to "draw him out" on federal politics and his highhanded attitude toward Congress. I thought some of the things I said were rather fine. But he merely looked around at me, at distant intervals, something as I have seen a benignant old cat look around to see which kitten was meddling with her

A young Samuel Clemens, traveling the world, Constantinople 1867

tail. By and by I subsided into an indignant silence, and so sat until the end, hot and flushed, and execrating him in my heart for an ignorant savage. But he was calm. His conversation with those gentlemen flowed on as sweetly and peacefully and musically as any summer brook. When the audience was ended and we were retiring from the presence, he put his hand on my head, beamed down on me in an admiring way and said to my brother:

"Ah—your child, I presume? Boy or girl?" (97)

Samuel Langhorne Clemens at home sometime before 1910

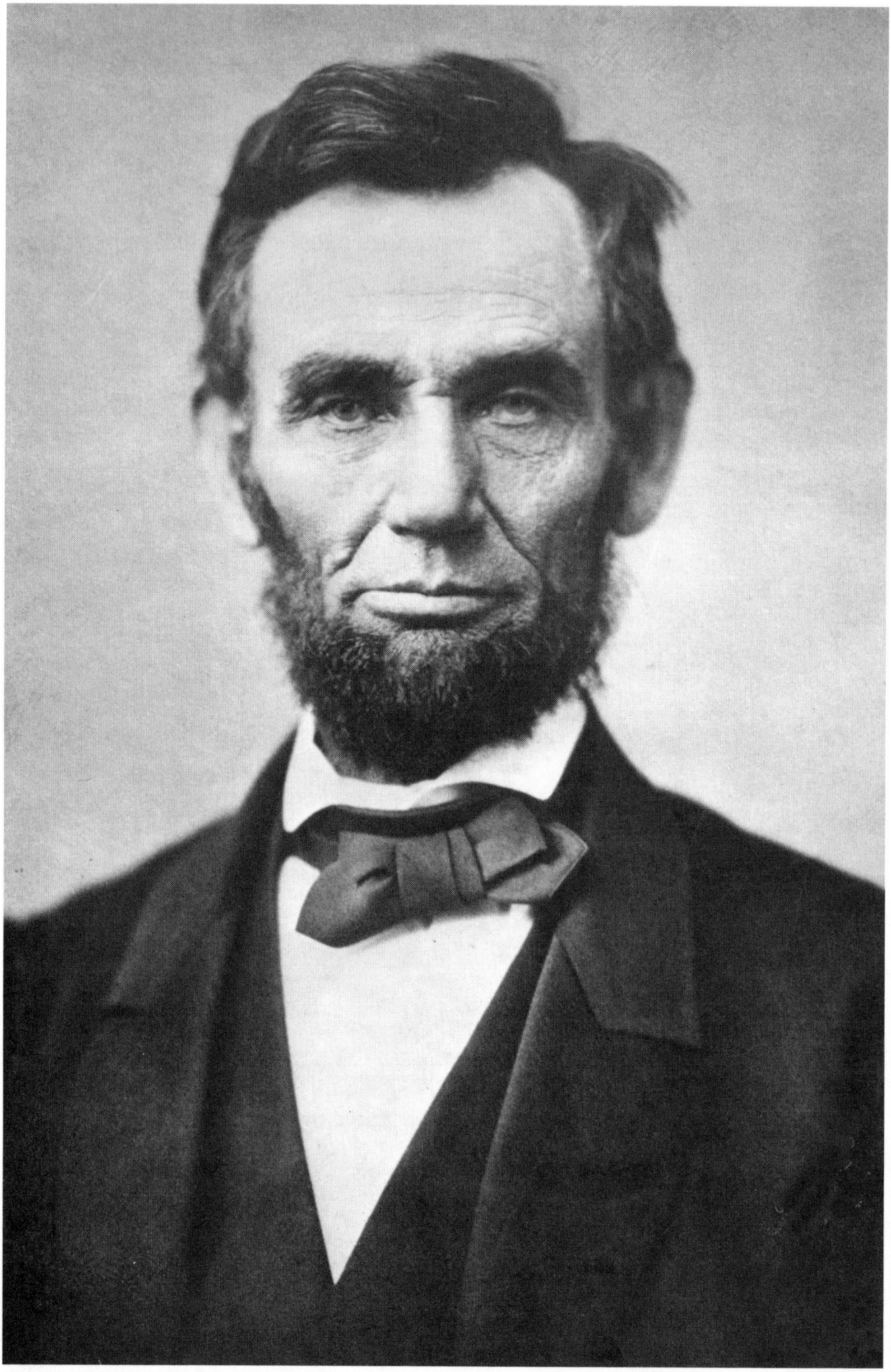

President Abraham Lincoln

1863

When Abraham Lincoln was elected president in 1860, seven Southern states responded to the outcome of the election by seceding. Not long after Lincoln's inauguration, shots were fired on Fort Sumter, and the Civil War began. Lincoln didn't approve of what was going on in Utah, but he had bigger things to worry about during his presidency—like preserving the Union—and decided that bothering the Saints wasn't worth the trouble.

>When I was a boy on the farm in Illinois there was a great deal of timber on the farm which we had to clear away. Occasionally we would come to a log which had fallen down. It was too hard to split, too wet to burn and too heavy to move, so we plowed around it. That's what I intend to do with the Mormons. You go back and tell Brigham Young that if he will let me alone I will let him alone. (In Preston Nibley, *Brigham Young: The Man and His Work*, 369)

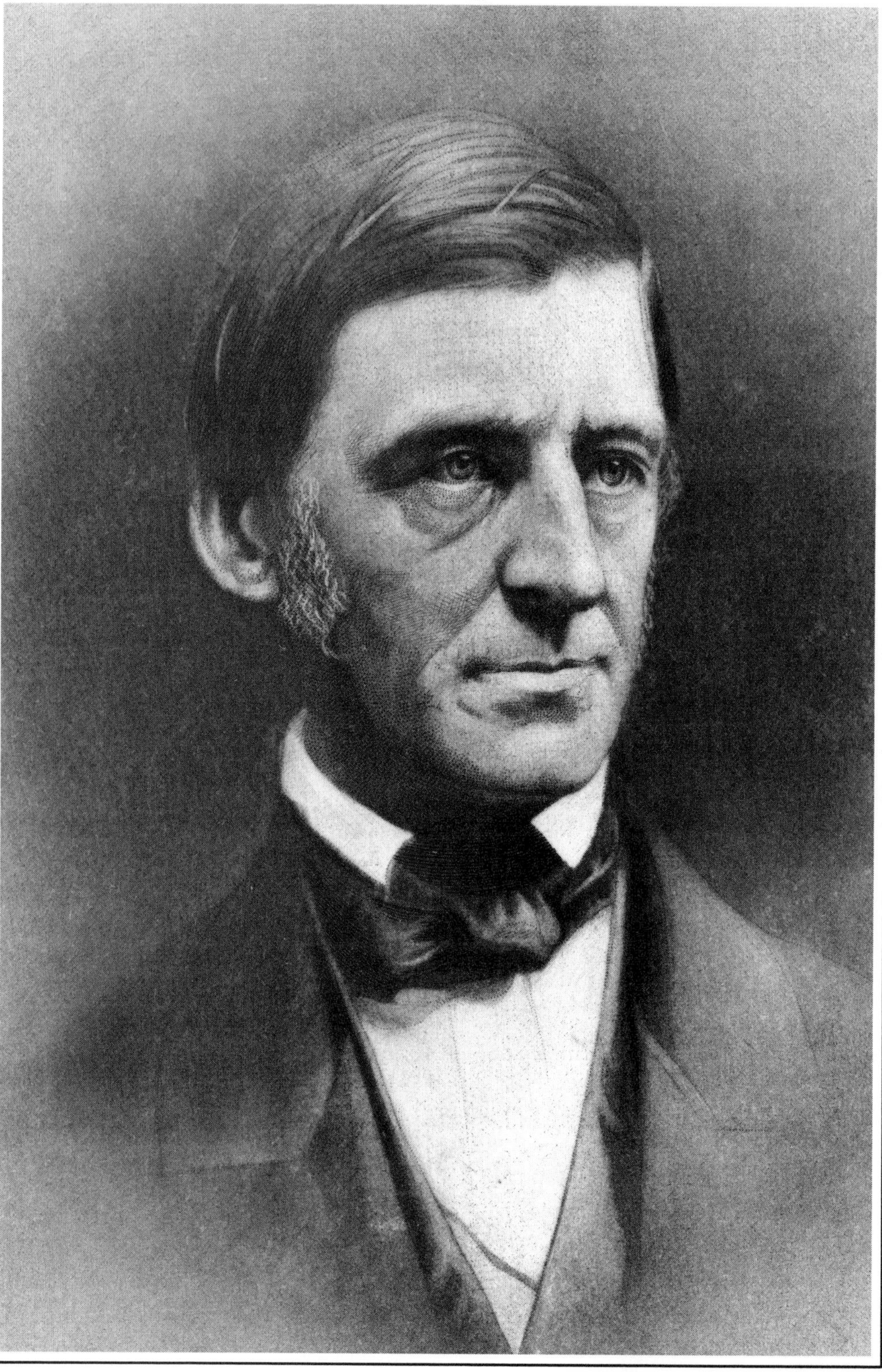

Ralph Waldo Emerson

1863

Famed American essayist and poet Ralph Waldo Emerson started his career as a Unitarian pastor. As a writer, he explored religion, culture, and especially the ideas of transcendentalism—a philosophy valuing nature and intuition over empirical evidence. In 1871, Emerson visited Salt Lake on his way to San Francisco, but the visit apparently had little impact on him as he wrote almost nothing about that experience and had mentioned Mormons and Mormonism in the past only briefly, mostly in a negative context. He did, however, recognize Brigham Young's contribution to the world in the following journal entry.

> *Good out of evil.* One must thank the genius of Brigham Young for the creation of Salt Lake City,—an inestimable hospitality to the Overland Emigrants, and an efficient example to all men in the vast desert, teaching how to subdue and turn it to a habitable garden. (*Journals of Ralph Waldo Emerson,* 540)

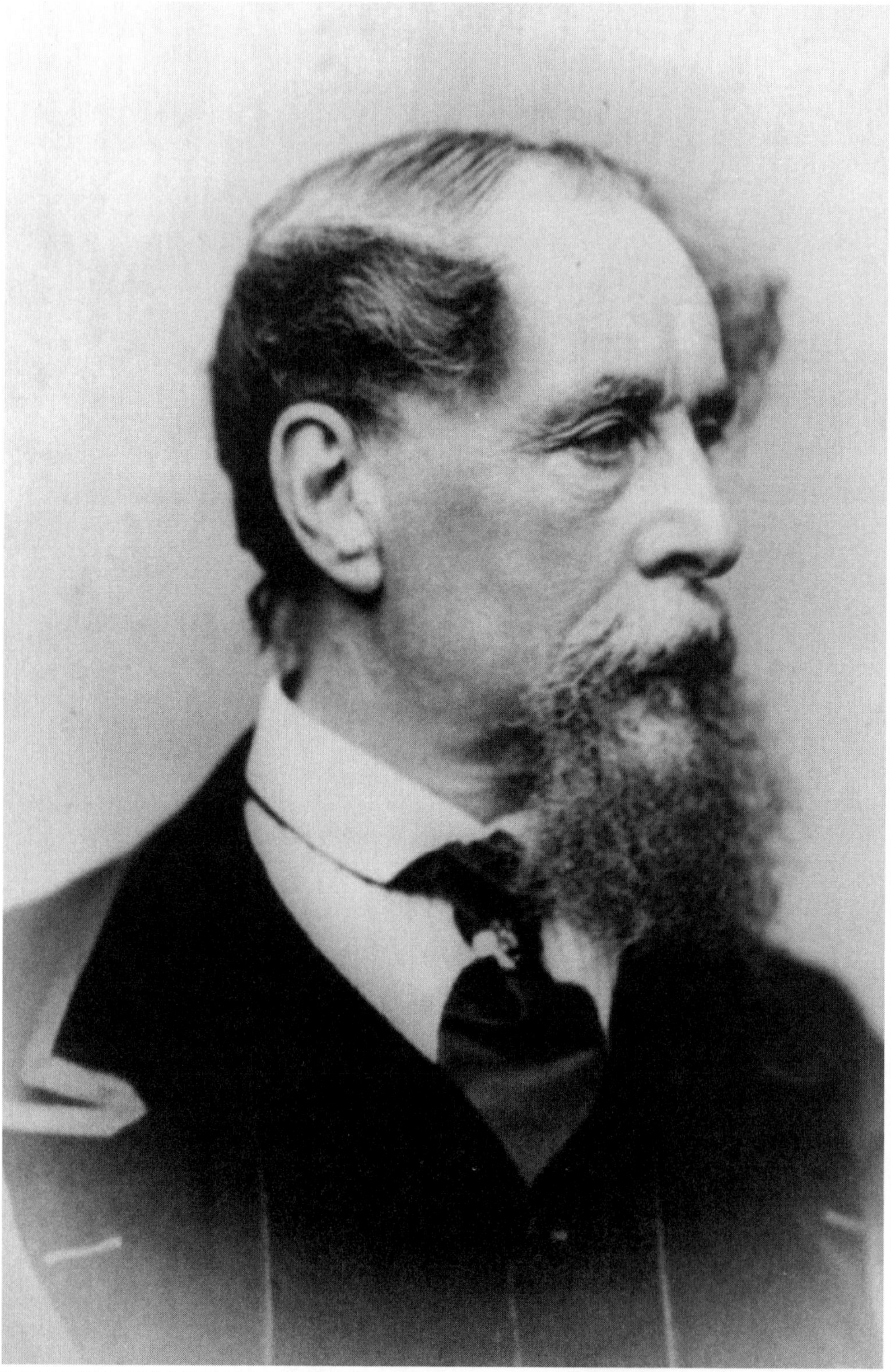

CHARLES DICKENS

1863

Beloved and best-selling author of Oliver Twist, A Tale of Two Cities, *and* A Christmas Carol, *Charles Dickens also wrote "The Uncommercial Traveller," a collection of articles on his travels and observations. One article reports his visit to the ship* Amazon *at its London dock to see what kind of people would be emigrating to America. What he found surprised him.*

BOUND FOR THE GREAT SALT LAKE

Behold me on my way to an Emigrant Ship, on a hot morning early in June. . . .

My Emigrant Ship lies broadside-on to the wharf. Two great gangways made of spars and planks connect her with the wharf; and up and down these gangways, perpetually crowding to and from and in and out, like ants, are the Emigrants who are going to sail in my Emigrant Ship. Some with cabbages, some with loaves of bread, some with cheese and butter, some with milk and beer, some with boxes, beds, and bundles, some with babies—nearly all with children—nearly all with bran-new tin cans for their daily allowance of water, uncomfortably suggestive of a tin flavour in the drink. To and from, up and down, aboard and ashore, swarming here and there and everywhere, my Emigrants. And still as the Dock Gate swings upon its hinges, cabs appear, and carts appear, and vans appear, bringing more of my Emigrants, with more cabbages, more loaves, more cheese and butter, more milk and beer, more boxes, beds, and bundles, more tin cans, and on those shipping investments accumulated compound interest of children.

I go aboard my Emigrant Ship. I go first to the great cabin, and find it in the usual condition of a cabin at that pass. Perspiring landsmen, with loose papers, and with pens and inkstands, pervade it; and the general appearance of things is as if the late Mr. Amazon's funeral had just come home from the cemetery, and the disconsolate Mrs. Amazon's trustees found the affairs in great disorder, and were looking high and low for the will. I go out on the poop-deck for air, and, surveying the emigrants on the deck below (indeed they are crowded all about me, up there too), find more pens and inkstands in action, and more papers, and interminable complication respecting accounts with individuals for tin cans and what not. But nobody is in an ill temper, nobody is the worse for drink, nobody swears an oath or uses a coarse word, nobody appears depressed, nobody is weeping; and down upon the deck, in every corner where it is possible to find a few square feet to kneel, crouch, or lie in, people in every unsuitable attitude for writing are writing letters.

Now, I have seen emigrant ships before this day in June. And these people are so strikingly different from all other people in like circumstances whom I have ever seen, that I wonder aloud, "What *would* a stranger suppose these emigrants to be!"

The vigilant bright face of the weather-browned captain of the Amazon is at my shoulder, and he says, "What, indeed! The most of these came aboard yesterday evening. They came from various parts of England in small parties that had never seen one another before. Yet they had not been a couple of hours on board when they established their own police, made their own regulations, and set their own watches at all the hatchways. Before nine o'clock the ship was as orderly and as quiet as a man-of-war."

I looked about me again, and saw the letter-writing going on with the most curious composure. Perfectly abstracted in the midst of the crowd—while great casks were swinging aloft, and being lowered into the hold; while hot agents were hurrying up and down, adjusting the interminable accounts; while two hundred strangers were searching everywhere for two hundred other strangers, and were asking questions about them of two hundred more; while the children played up and down all the steps, and in and out among all the people's legs, and were beheld, to the general dismay, toppling over all the dangerous places,—the letter-writers wrote on calmly. On the starboard side of the ship a grizzled man dictated a long letter to another grizzled man in an immense fur cap; which letter was of so profound a quality that it became necessary for the amanuensis at intervals to take off his fur cap in both his hands, for the ventilation of his brain, and stare at him who dictated, as a man of many mysteries who was worth looking at. On the larboard side a woman had covered a belaying-pin with a white cloth, to make a neat desk of it, and was sitting on a little box, writing with the deliberation of a bookkeeper. Down upon her breast on the planks of the deck at this woman's feet, with her head diving in under a beam of the bulwarks on that side, as an eligible place of refuge for her sheet of paper, a neat and pretty girl wrote for a good hour (she fainted at last), only rising to the surface occasionally for a dip of ink. Alongside the boat, close to me on the poop-deck, another girl, a fresh well-grown country girl, was writing another letter on the bare deck. Later in the day, when this self-same boat was filled with a choir who sang glees and catches for a long time, one of the singers, a girl, sang her part mechanically all the while, and wrote a letter in the bottom of the boat while doing so.

"A stranger would be puzzled to guess the right name for these people, Mr. Uncommercial," says the captain.

"Indeed he would."

"If you hadn't known, could you ever have supposed—?"

"How could I! I should have said they were in their degree, the pick and flower of England."

"So should I," says the captain.

"How many are they?"

"Eight hundred, in round numbers."

I went between-decks, where the families with children swarmed in the dark, where unavoidable confusion had been caused by the last arrivals, and where the confusion was increased by the little preparations for dinner that were going on in each group. A few women here and there had got lost, and were laughing at it, and asking their way to their own people, or out on deck again. A few of the poor children were crying; but otherwise the universal cheerfulness was amazing. "We shall shake down by to-morrow." "We shall come all right in a day or so." "We shall have more light at sea." Such phrases I heard everywhere, as I groped my way among chests and barrels and beams and unstored cargo and ring-bolts and Emigrants, down to the lower deck, and thence up to the light of day again and to my former station.

Surely an extraordinary people in their power of self-abstraction! All the former letter-writers were still writing calmly, and many more letter-writers had broken out in my absence. A boy with a bag of books in his hand and a slate under his arm emerged from below, concentrated himself in my neighbourhood (espying a convenient skylight for his purpose), and went to work at a sum as if he were stone-deaf. A father and mother and several young children, on the main-deck below me, had formed a family circle close to the foot of the crowded restless gangway, where the children made a nest for themselves in a coil of rope, and the father and mother, she suckling the youngest, discussed family affairs as peaceably as if they were in perfect retirement. I think the most noticeable characteristic in the eight hundred as a mass, was their exemption from hurry.

Eight hundred what? "Geese, villain?"

EIGHT HUNDRED MORMONS. I, Uncommercial Traveler for the firm of Human Interest Brothers, had come aboard this Emigrant Ship to see what Eight Hundred Latter-day Saints were like: and I found them (to the rout and overthrow of all my expectations) like what I now describe with scrupulous exactness.

The Mormon Agent who had been active in getting them together, and in making the contract with my friends, the owners of the ship, to take them as far as New York on their way to the Great Salt Lake, was pointed out to me. A compactly-made handsome man in black, rather short, with rich-brown hair and beard, and clear bright eyes. From his speech, I should set him down as American. Probably, a man who had "knocked

Prolific British author Charles Dickens in 1867

about the world" pretty much. A man with a frank open manner, and unshrinking look; withal a man of great quickness. I believe he was wholly ignorant of my Uncommercial individuality, and consequently of my immense Uncommercial importance.

UNCOMMERCIAL. These are a very fine set of people you have brought together here.

MORMON AGENT. Yes, sir, they are a very fine set of people.

UNCOMMERCIAL (looking about). Indeed, I think it would be difficult to find eight hundred people together anywhere else, and find so much beauty and so much strength and capacity for work among them.

MORMON AGENT (not looking about, but looking steadily at Uncommercial). I think so.— We sent out about a thousand more, yes'day, from Liverpool.

UNCOMMERCIAL. You are not going with these emigrants?

MORMON AGENT. No, sir. I remain.

UNCOMMERCIAL. But you have been in the Mormon Territory?

MORMON AGENT. Yes; I left Utah about three years ago.

UNCOMMERCIAL. It is surprising to me that these people are all so cheery, and make so little of the immense distance before them.

MORMON AGENT. Well, you see; many of 'em have friends out at Utah, and many of 'em look forward to meeting friends on the way.

UNCOMMERCIAL. On the way?

MORMON AGENT. This way 'tis. This ship lands 'em in New York City. Then they go on by rail right away beyond St. Louis, to that part of the banks of the Missouri where they strike the Plains. There wagons from the settlement meet 'em to bear 'em company on their journey 'cross,—twelve hundred miles, about. Industrious people who come out to the settlement soon get wagons of their own, and so the friends of some of these will come down in their own wagons to meet 'em. They look forward to that greatly.

It is surprising to me that these people are all so cheery

UNCOMMERCIAL. On their long journey across the desert, do you arm them?

MORMON AGENT. Mostly you would find they have arms of some kind or another already with them. Such as had not arms we should arm across the Plains, for the general protection and defence.

UNCOMMERCIAL. Will these wagons bring down any produce to the Missouri?

MORMON AGENT. Well, since the war broke out, we've taken to growing cotton, and they'll likely bring down cotton to be exchanged for machinery. We want machinery. Also we have taken to growing indigo, which is a fine commodity for profit. It has been found that the climate on the further side of the Great Salt Lake suits well for raising indigo.

UNCOMMERCIAL. I am told that these people now on board are principally from the South of England.

MORMON AGENT. And from Wales. That's true.

UNCOMMERCIAL. Do you get many Scotch?

MORMON AGENT. Not many.

UNCOMMERCIAL. Highlanders, for instance?

MORMON AGENT. No, not Highlanders. They ain't interested enough in universal brotherhood and peace and good will.

UNCOMMERCIAL. The old fighting blood is strong in them?

MORMON AGENT. Well, yes. And besides, they've no faith.

UNCOMMERCIAL. (who has been burning to get at the Prophet Joe Smith, and seems to discover an opening). Faith in—

MORMON AGENT. (far too many for Uncommercial). Well—In anything!

Similarly on this same head, the Uncommercial underwent discomfiture from a Wiltshire labourer,— a simple, fresh-coloured farm-labourer, of eight-and-thirty, who at one time stood beside him looking on at new arrivals, and with whom he held this dialogue:

UNCOMMERCIAL. Would you mind my asking you what part of the country you come from?

WILTSHIRE. Not a bit. Theer! (exultingly). I've worked all my life o' Salisbury Plain, right under the shadder o' Stonehenge. You mightn't think it, but I haive.

UNCOMMERCIAL. And a pleasant country too.

WILTSHIRE. Ah! 'Tis a pleasant country.

UNCOMMERCIAL. Have you any family on board?

WILTSHIRE. Two children—boy and gal. I am a widderer, I am, and I'm going out alonger my boy and gal. That's my gal, and she's a fine gal o' sixteen (pointing out the girl who is writing by the boat). I'll go and fetch my boy. I'd like to show you my boy. (Here Wiltshire disappears, and presently comes back with a big shy boy of twelve, in a superabundance of boots, who is not at all glad to be presented.) He is a fine boy, too, and a boy fur to work! (Boy having undutifully bolted, Wiltshire drops him.)

UNCOMMERCIAL. It must cost you a great deal of money to go so far, three strong.

WILTSHIRE. A power of money. Theer! Eight shillen a week, eight shillen a week, eight shillen a week, put by out of the week's wages for ever so long.

UNCOMMERCIAL. I wonder how you did it.

WILTSHIRE. (recognising in this a kindred spirit). See theer now! I wonder how I done it! But what with a bit o' subscription heer, and what with a bit o' help theer, it were done at last, though I don't hardly know how. Then it were unfort'net for us, you see, as we got kep' in Bristol so long—nigh a fortnight, it were—on accounts of a mistake wi' Brother Halliday. Swaller'd up money, it did, when we might have come straight on.

UNCOMMERCIAL. (delicately approaching Joe Smith). You are of the Mormon religion, of course?

WILTSHIRE. (confidently). Oh, yes, I'm a Mormon. (Then reflectively.) I'm a Mormon. (Then, looking round the ship, feigns to descry a particular friend in an empty spot, and evades the Uncommercial for evermore.)

After a noontide pause for dinner, during which my Emigrants were nearly all between-decks, and the Amazon looked deserted, a general muster took place. The muster was for the ceremony of passing the government inspector and the doctor. Those authorities held their temporary state amidships, by a cask or two; and, knowing that the whole Eight Hundred emigrants must come face to face with them, I took my station behind the two. They knew nothing whatever of me, I believe; and my testimony to the unpretending gentleness and good-nature with which they discharged their duty, may be of the greater worth. There was not the slightest flavour of the Circumlocution Office about their proceedings.

The emigrants were now all on deck. They were densely crowded aft, and swarmed upon the poop-deck like bees. Two or three Mormon agents stood ready to hand them on to the Inspector, and to hand them forward when they had passed. By what successful means, a special aptitude for organisation had been infused into these people, I am, of course, unable to report. But I know that, even now, there was no disorder, hurry, or difficulty.

Oh, yes, I'm a Mormon. . . . I'm a Mormon.

All being ready, the first group are handed on. That member of the party who is entrusted with the passenger ticket for the whole, has been warned by one of the agents to have it ready, and here it is in his hand. In every instance through the whole Eight Hundred, without an exception, this paper is always ready.

INSPECTOR (reading the ticket). Jessie Jobson, Sophronia Jobson, Jessie Jobson again, Matilda Jobson, William Jobson, Jane Jobson, Matilda

Jobson again, Brigham Jobson, Leonardo Jobson, and Orson Jobson. Are you all here? (glancing at the party over his spectacles).

JESSE JOBSON NUMBER TWO. All here, sir.

This group is composed of an old grandfather and grandmother, their married son and his wife, and their family of children. Orson Jobson is a little child asleep in his mother's arms. The doctor, with a kind word or so, lifts up the corner of the mother's shawl, looks at the child's face, and touches the little clenched hand. If we were all as well as Orson Jobson, doctoring would be a poor profession.

INSPECTOR. Quite right, Jessie Jobson. Take your ticket, Jessie, and pass on.

And away they go. Mormon agent, skilful and quiet, hands them on. Mormon agent, skilful and quiet, hands next party up.

INSPECTOR (reading ticket again). Susannah Cleverly and William Cleverly. Brother and sister, eh?

SISTER (young woman of business, hustling slow brother). Yes, sir.

INSPECTOR. Very good, Susannah Cleverly. Take your ticket, Susannah, and take care of it.

And away they go. . . .

INSPECTOR (taking ticket again). Anastatia Weedle.

ANASTATIA (a pretty girl, in a bright garibaldi, this morning elected by universal suffrage the Beauty of the Ship). That is me, sir.

INSPECTOR. Going alone, Anastatia?

ANASTATIA (shaking her curls). I am with Mrs. Jobson, sir, but I've got separated for the moment.

INSPECTOR. Oh! You are with the Jobsons? Quite right. That'll do, Miss Weedle. Don't lose your ticket.

Away she goes, and joins the Jobsons who are waiting for her, and stoops and kisses Brigham Jobson—who appears to be considered too young for the purpose by several Mormons rising twenty, who are looking on. Before her extensive skirts have departed from the casks, a decent widow stands there with four children, and so the roll goes.

The faces of some of the Welsh people, among whom there were many old persons, were certainly the least intelligent. Some of these emigrants would have bungled sorely, but for the directing hand that was always ready. The intelligence here was unquestionably of a low order, and the heads were of a poor type. Generally the case was the reverse. There were many worn faces bearing traces of patient poverty and hard work, and there was great steadiness of purpose and much undemonstrative self-respect among the class. A few young men were going singly. Several girls were going two or three together. These latter I found it very difficult to refer back, in my mind, to their relinquished homes and pursuits. Perhaps they were more like country milliners, and pupil teachers rather tawdrily dressed, than any other classes of young women. I noticed, among many other ornaments worn, more than one photograph-brooch of the Princess of Wales, and also of the late Prince Consort. Some single women of from thirty to forty, whom one might suppose to be embroiderers, or straw-bonnet makers, were obviously going out in quest of husbands, as finer ladies go to India. That they had any distinct notions of a plurality of husbands or wives, I do not believe. To suppose the family groups of whom the majority of emigrants were composed polygamically possessed would be to suppose an absurdity manifest to any one who saw the fathers and mothers.

I should say (I had no means of ascertaining the fact) that the most familiar kinds of handicraft trades were represented here. Farm labourers, shepherds, and the like, had their full share of representation, but I doubt if they preponderated. It was interesting to see how the leading spirit in the family circle never failed to show itself, even in the simple process of answering to the names as they were called, and checking off the owners of the names. Sometimes it was the father, much oftener the mother, sometimes a quick little girl second or third in order of seniority. It seemed to occur for the first time to some heavy fathers, what large families they had; and their eyes rolled about, during the calling of the list, as if they half misdoubted some other family to have been smuggled into their own. Among all the fine handsome children, I observed but two with marks upon their necks that were probably scrofulous. Out of the whole number of emigrants, but one old woman was temporarily set aside by the doctor, on suspicion of fever; but even she afterwards obtained a clean bill of health.

When all had "passed," and the afternoon began to wear on, a black box became visible on deck, which box was in charge of certain personages also in black, of whom only one had the conventional air of an itinerant preacher. This box contained a supply of hymn-books, neatly printed and got up, published at Liverpool, and also in London at the "Latter-Day Saints' Book Depot, 30, Florence-street." Some copies were handsomely bound; the plainer were the more in request, and many were bought. The title ran, "Sacred Hymns and Spiritual Songs for the Church of Jesus Church (sic) of Latter-Day Saints." The Preface, dated Manchester, 1840, ran thus: "The Saints in this country have been very desirous for a Hymn-book adapted to their faith and worship, that they might sing the truth with an understanding heart, and express their praise joy and gratitude in songs adapted to the New and Everlasting Covenant. In accordance with their wishes, we have selected the following volume, which we hope will prove acceptable until a greater variety can be added. With sentiments of high consideration and esteem, we subscribe ourselves your brethren in the New and Everlasting Covenant, BRIGHAM YOUNG, PARLEY P. PRATT, JOHN TAYLOR." From this book—by no means explanatory to myself of the New and Everlasting Covenant, and not at all making my heart an understanding one on the subject of that mystery—a hymn was sung, which did not attract any great amount

Charles Dickens (1812–1870)—the most popular writer of the Victorian Age

of attention, and was supported by a rather select circle. But the choir in the boat was very popular and pleasant; and there was to have been a Band, only the Cornet was late in coming on board. In the course of the afternoon, a mother appeared from shore, in search of her daughter, "who had run away with the Mormons." She received every assistance from the Inspector, but her daughter was not found to be on board. The Saints did not seem to me particularly interested in finding her.

Towards five o'clock, the galley became full of tea-kettles, and an agreeable fragrance of tea pervaded the ship. There was no scrambling or jostling for the hot water, no ill-humour, no quarrelling. As the Amazon was to sail with the next tide, and as it would not be high water before two o'clock in the morning, I left her with her tea in full action, and her idle steam tug lying by, deputing steam and smoke for the time being to the tea-kettles.

I afterwards learned that a dispatch was sent home by the captain, before he struck out into the wide Atlantic, highly extolling the behaviour of these Emigrants, and the perfect order and propriety of all their social arrangements. What is in store for the poor people on the shores of the Great Salt Lake, what happy delusions they are labouring under now, on what miserable blindness their eyes may be opened then, I do not pretend to say. But I went on board their ship to bear testimony against them if they deserved it, as I fully believed they would; to my great astonishment they did not deserve it; and my predispositions and tendencies must not affect me as an honest witness. I went over the Amazon's side, feeling it impossible to deny that, so far, some remarkable influence had produced a remarkable result, which better-known influences have often missed.[1]

[1] After this Uncommercial Journey was printed, I happened to mention the experience it describes to Mr. Monckton Milnes, M. P. That gentleman then showed me an article of his writing, in *The Edinburgh Review* for January, 1862, which is highly remarkable for its philosophical and literary research concerning these Latter-Day Saints. I find in it the following sentences: "The Select Committee of the House of Commons on emigrant ships for 1854 summoned the Mormon agent and passenger broker before it, and came to the conclusion that no ships under the provisions of the 'Passengers Act' could be depended upon for comfort and security in the same degree as those under his administration. The Mormon ship is a Family under strong and accepted discipline, with every provision for comfort, decorum, and internal peace." (Dickens, *The Uncommercial Traveller*, 198–210)

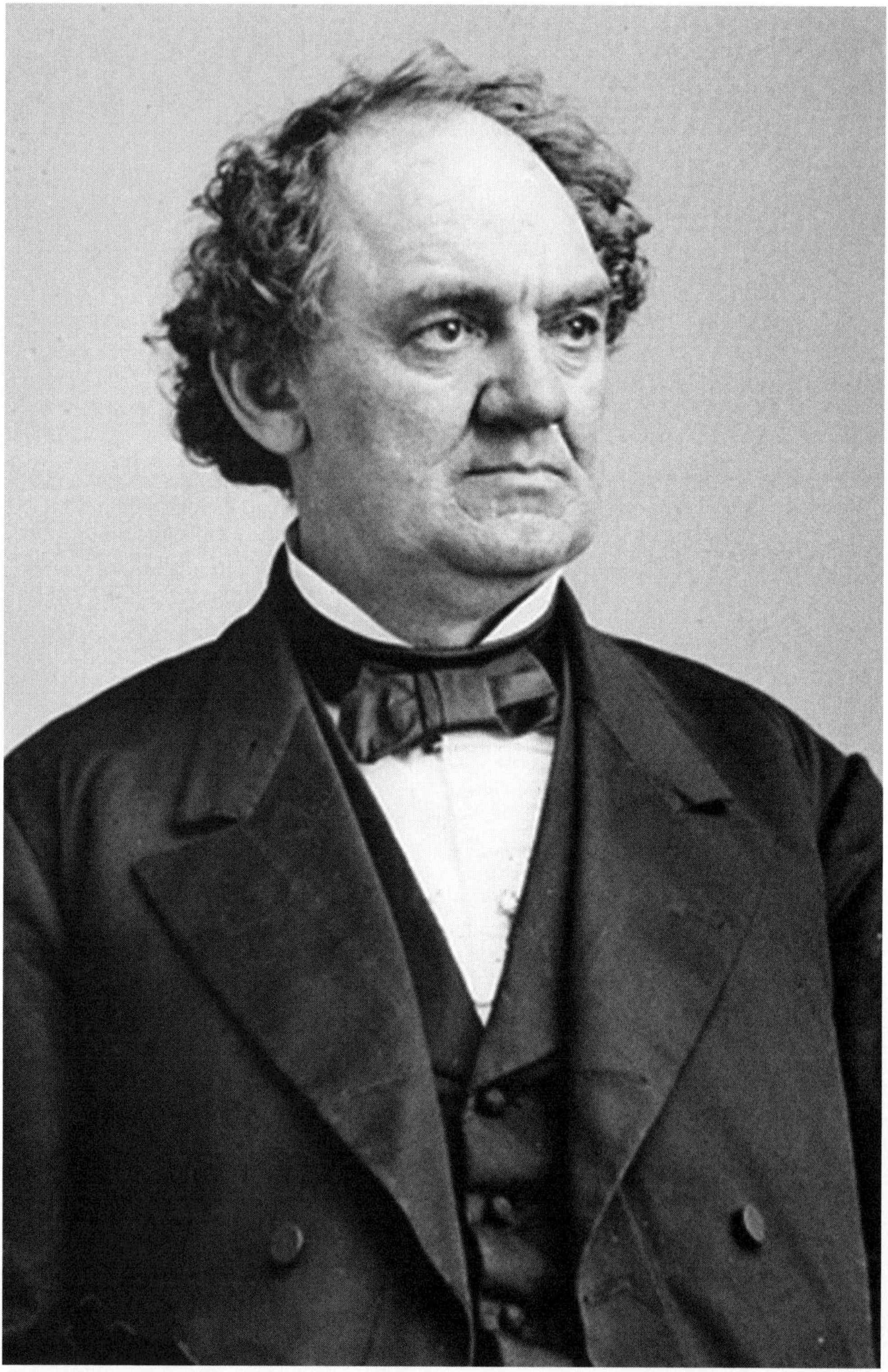

P. T. Barnum

1868

P. T. Barnum, the world's greatest showman, didn't enter the circus business he's so well remembered for until late in his life. First, he made a fortune from building and managing entertaining museums. After his second museum burned down in March of 1868, he "retired." But he soon grew bored of reading, chess playing, and concert going. He was therefore delighted when English friends of his asked him to be their guide on a journey around America. In April they passed through Utah.

In April we made up a small, congenial party of ladies and gentlemen, and visited California via the Union and Central Pacific Railroads.

We journeyed leisurely, and I lectured in Council Bluffs, Omaha and Salt Lake City, where amongst my audience were a dozen or so of Brigham Young's wives and scores of his children. By invitation, I called with my friends on President Young at the Bee-Hive. He received us very cordially, asked us many questions, and promptly answered ours.

"Barnum," said he, "what will you give to exhibit me in New York and the eastern cities?"

"Well, Mr. President," I replied, "I'll give you half the receipts, which I will guarantee shall be

Phineas Taylor "P. T." Barnum shown with General Tom Thumb

$200,000 per year, for I consider you the best show in America."

"Why did you not secure me some years ago when I was of no consequence?" he continued.

"Because, you would not have 'drawn' at that time," I answered.

Brigham smiled and said, "I would like right well to spend a few hours with you, if you could come when I am disengaged." I thanked him, and told him I guessed I should enjoy it; but visitors were crowding into his reception-room, and we withdrew. (Phineas Taylor Barnum, *Struggles and Triumphs,* 282)

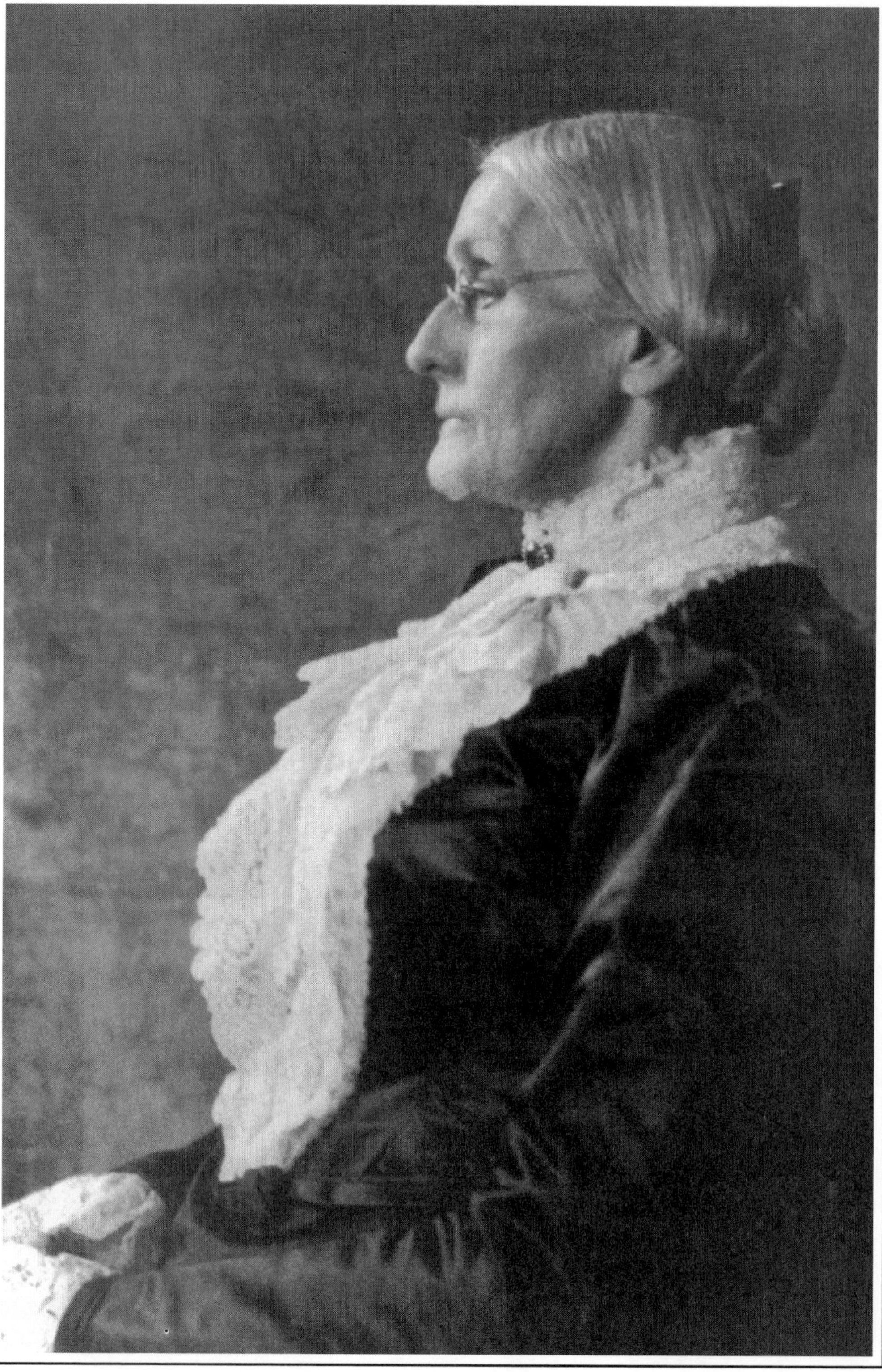

Susan B. Anthony

1871

Susan B. Anthony emerged as a leader in the women's suffrage movement when, as a teacher, she fought for equal pay and college education for women. Later she founded a women's organization advocating temperance when the men's temperance organization refused to allow her to participate. Elizabeth Cady Stanton joined Anthony's group and became a lifelong friend and co-leader in the political movement for women's rights. The two visited Utah in June of 1871, where they observed conditions and became friends with the Mormon women. Polygamy wasn't a big issue to Anthony and Stanton. As far as they were concerned, the major problem women had was economic dependence, and this problem was the same whether in monogamous or polygamous households.

> As they sang their songs of freedom, poured out their rejoicings . . . and told of the beatitudes of soul-to-soul communion with the All-Father, my heart was steeped in deepest sympathy with the women around me and, rising at an opportune pause, I asked if a woman and a stranger might be permitted to say a word. At once the entire circle of men on the platform rose and beckoned me forward; and, with a Quaker inspiration not

Susan B. Anthony—women's suffrage leader who visited Utah in the nineteenth century

to be repeated, much less put on paper, I asked those men, bubbling over with the divine spirit of freedom for themselves, if they had thought whether the women of their households were to-day rejoicing in like manner? I can not tell what I said—only this I know, that young and beautiful, old and wrinkled women alike wept, and men said, "I wanted to get out-of-doors where I could shout." (Katharine Susan Anthony, *Susan B. Anthony,* 261)

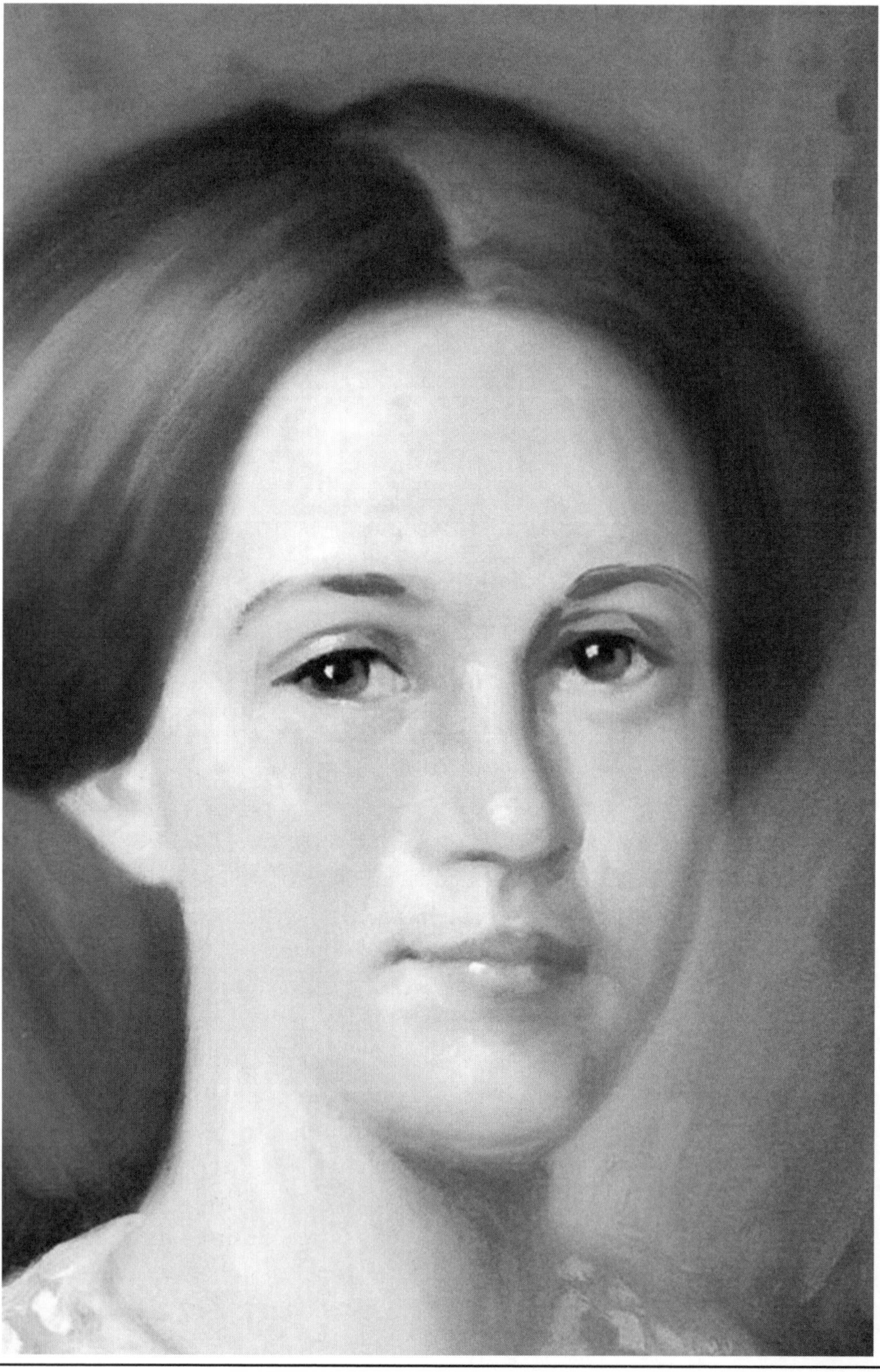

Elizabeth Kane

1872

Colonel Thomas Kane intervened with the U.S. government several times on behalf of the Mormons. For that the Mormons were forever grateful. So when he, his wife Elizabeth, and their two sons visited Brigham Young in the fall of 1872, they came as friends and were guests of President Young on his journey to St. George. Along the way the party stayed in several Mormon towns, in several Mormon homes. Elizabeth wrote of the journey and their visit in each home.

At every one of the places we stayed on this journey, we had prayers immediately after the dinner-supper, and prayers again before breakfast. No one was excused; wives, daughters, hired men and women, all shuffled in. The Mormons do not read from the Bible, but kneel at once, while the head of the household or an honored guest prays aloud, beginning, as I noticed on this occasion, instead of ending, "In the name of Thy Son, our Saviour Jesus Christ, Father, we ask," etc. I do not think they as often say, "If it be Thy Will," as we do, but simply pray for the blessings they want, expecting they will be given or withheld, as God knows best. Though I do remember Brigham

Young's once praying for the restoration and healing of the sick "if not appointed unto death." They spend very little time in ascriptions, but ask for what they need and thank Him for what He has given—with surprising fluency and details. (Elizabeth Kane, *Twelve Mormon Homes,* 18–19)

At another watering-place, Santaquin, I think, somewhat above the general level of the plain, we saw quite a number of white-topped wagons slowly toiling along the dusty track below us. Some lighter ones turned aside, as we ourselves frequently did, to drive through the aromatic sage-brush. It scarcely afforded more obstruction to the wheels than grass would have done. But while we were standing at a watering-trough, up rolled one of the coaches of the Gilmore Stage line. I noticed the half-tipsy mirth on the countenances of the driver and of the two red-faced passengers, who were leaning out of the window watching his movements. By a skilfully-given pull of the reins, he steered his heavy wagon right against the hub of our front wheel, and then drove off laughing. Unfortunately for the joke, however, the villagers beyond stopped his team, and he came back, crestfallen, to apologize. It was undoubtedly meant as an insult to the Mormon leader, in whose well-known carriage, however, the only Gentiles of the party happened to be seated. President Young received his excuses with dignity, instead of "blowing him up," as a more impetuous friend of mine was ready to do. Our carriage was examined, and pronounced still fit for work; but it took some hours at our next stopping-place to repair the damage. The people of the village complained that this was a favorite amusement of the coaches near this point, where the Mormon travel coincides with that of the Nevada mining regions. (21–22)

I could see little of Nephi in the gathering darkness: it was evidently smaller than Provo. The carriages halted on entering the town, and separated company. Ours was driven rapidly up a cross-street to a plain adobe house, standing by itself. Lights shone from every door and window; the father of the family stood waiting to help us out of the carriage, and the wives and children greeted us warmly as we crossed the threshold.

We were first ushered into a large bedroom on the ground floor, where a superb pitch-pine fire was blazing; and two well-cushioned rocking-chairs were drawn forward for us, while half a dozen hospitable children took off my boys' wrappings, as the mother disembarrassed me of mine.

Then we were left to rest, and begged to feel ourselves at home.

Our present entertainers, the Steerforths, were English people. There were two wives, and a number of children, girls of all sizes down to the smallest elf that ever walked, and one sturdy open-faced boy, who speedily "fellow-shipped" with my little lads, and carried them off, after supper, to the great kitchen to see their playmate, Lehi, the Indian boy.

After supper!—To this day, when we have any special dainty at home, Evan and Will exclaim that it reminds them of the Steerforths', and describe the cozy dining-room with the warm fire-light playing on the table-equipage, and the various good things that composed, in Yorkshire style, the hungry little travelers' "tea-dinner."

One of the wives sat down to table, and one waited upon us, with the aid of the two elder girls. There was a young schoolmaster there, too, who had made his home with the Steerforths since his parents died, and whose love of their quiet domestic life was duly praised by the Mistresses S. when he left the room. But I thought that the sweet face of "our eldest"— "Noe," I think they call her—might perhaps share the credit of the long ten-mile ride on Friday evening from his school to Nephi, and the starlight journey back which it cost the youthful pedagogue on Monday morning.

It was difficult not to be influenced by their simple kindliness of heart and unaffected enthusiasm.

My intercourse with the Steerforths made a strong impression on me. We stayed longer at their house than at any other on this tour, and it was difficult not to be influenced by their simple kindliness of heart and unaffected enthusiasm.

Our conversation the evening of our arrival turned chiefly on our hostesses' experience of pioneer life. Mrs. Mary was the chief speaker, but Mrs. Sarah, a pale little lady, dark-haired and black-eyed, put in a quiet word of acquiescence, or suggested an anecdote now and then. She was from Yorkshire. Mrs. Mary was a Herefordshire woman, tall, rosy, brown-haired, and blue-eyed.

I wonder whether the Mormon men evince any marked peculiarity of taste in the selection of wives. Widowers with us are wont to profess that they discern a resemblance in the lady upon whom a second choice falls, to the dear departed. I asked a Mormon woman at Salt Lake how it was, and she answered that, in her opinion, men had no taste. "In our case," she said, "there are five of us unusually tall, and two very short; but the rest (she did not say how many there were) are of an ordinary height, and we are all different in looks, disposition, and age."

In the Steerforth ménage, the wives were exceedingly unlike each other. The husband was of a Manx family, long resident in Yorkshire. He had joined the Mormons in early youth with his mother, and they had been disowned by his family, well-to-do English people. He had prospered so well in Utah, however, that the family had now made overtures of reconciliation, and a bachelor "Uncle Lillivick" was coming to make Nephi a visit. (26–29)

<hr />

After breakfast I attended a Mormon meeting for the first time. I wondered whether Mr. Steerforth would walk to church alone, or between his wives. But they both accompanied me, while their joint husband (!) formed one of a group who escorted T. So there was no test of preference like that which mocks the tomb of Lord Burleigh. We soon mingled with a stream of neatly-dressed people all going the same way; my children undevoutly rambling from one side of the road to the other. They called my attention to a tamed magpie, whose remarks the little Steerforths declared to be worth hearing. But we paused in vain; he would not show off. I had not known that the magpie was a native of Utah; I had supposed him a peculiarly English bird.

We passed a heap of smouldering brands—sticks and ragged strips of cedar-bark. I had fancied that a fire of "cedarn-wood" would give out a scent like sandal-wood. The perfume resembled that of the fustiest of greasy woolen clothes, and was strong enough to poison the sweet air for quite a distance.

I got rid of more than one preconceived idea that morning; of none more completely than the prevailing error respecting the looks of a congregation of Mormon women. I was so placed that I had a good opportunity to look around, and began at once to seek for the "hopeless, dissatisfied, worn" expression travelers' books had bidden me read on their faces.

But I found that they wore very much the same countenances as the American women of any large rustic and village congregation.

As we grow older, most of us pass through trials enough to score their marks upon cheek and brow; but ill-health and ill-temper plough furrows quite as deep as guilt or misfortune. Take your own congregation, the sad histories of so many of whose members you know, and see whether you can read the tragedies of their lives beneath the composed Sunday expression their faces wear. Happy or unhappy, *I* could not read histories on the upturned faces at Nephi. I looked on old women's sunburned and wrinkled visages, half-hidden in their clean sunbonnets; decent, matronly countenances framed in big old-fashioned bonnets; bright, young eyes and rosy cheeks under coquettish round hats—you might see thousands of women resembling them in our country churches.

The irrepressible baby was present in greater force than with us, and the element young man wonderfully largely represented. This is always observable in Utah meetings. (45–47)

The mistress of the mansion showed herself in the door-way; a large, loosely-built matron, "standing with reluctant feet" on the uninteresting border-land between middle and old age.

She rather made way for us to enter, than entreated us. We found her parlor in keeping with the exterior of the house, and heated almost to suffocation by a large sheet-iron stove. She sat with us a few moments, lamenting that her children were all married and gone; lamenting the trouble of housekeeping unaided; and by inference lamenting the trouble of entertaining *me*. I condoled with her most sincerely, regretting her latest trouble perhaps even more than she did.

After she withdrew to prepare our meal, a son of hers came in to call on T. This gentleman had frequently acted as sub Indian agent, and a quintette of Indians, emboldened by his presence, followed him into the room. When Mrs. Q. called us to supper, these gentry rose to accompany us. I looked helplessly at her. She said a few words in their dialect, which made them at once squat down again, huddling their blankets round them, with a pleasanter look on their dark faces than they had yet worn.

"What did your mother say to those men, Mr. Q.?" I asked, curiously.

"She said 'These strangers came first, and I have only cooked enough for them; but your meal is on the fire cooking now, and I will call you as soon as it is ready.'"

"Will she really do that, or just give them scraps at the kitchen-door?" I pursued, thinking of "cold-victual" beggars at home.

"*Our* Pah-vants know how to behave," he answered, with the pride of the Kirkbride in his own lunatics. "Mother will serve them just as she does you, and give them a place at her table."

And so she did. I saw her placing clean plates, knives, and forks for them, and waiting behind their chairs, while they ate with perfect propriety. She rose a hundred per cent. in my opinion. (71–72)

I stayed at one of Bishop Collister's cottages in the orchard the next time I visited Fillmore.

The Mormons say that frost after frost killed the peach-trees and cut the apple-trees to the ground when they first made a settlement in the place, and did so year after year. Any reasonable people would have given up trying to produce fruit; but the Mormons are quite *un*reasonable in matters of faith, and some brother or sister had had it revealed, or had a vision, or "felt to prophesy" that it would yet be noted among the towns of Utah for its fruits. They persevered, and so I know what perfectly delicious apples they now harvest. Our bedroom at Fillmore had a great basket full of them, golden and rosy, sweet and tart, pippins and Spitzenbergs; with which we amused our palates between meals, and filled every nook in the carriage next day.

Mother will serve them just as she does you, and give them a place at her table.

My new hostess was, I believe, a daughter of my first one. What a pretty creature she was! Tall and graceful; with the loveliest of dark eyes! And she had three sweet little children—"three left out of seven." Her husband had lost eleven out of his twenty-eight children. Wife Mary had borne him seven, Caroline twelve, and Helen nine.

These numbers are not unusual in Utah, nor were they among the Puritans, our ancestors. But their *past* experience, at all events, gives the Mormons no right to claim that the mothers of families rear a greater number proportionately than with us. More children may have been born to each mother; but in each new settlement in Utah, the first stirring of the soil, the chemical exhalations, the fierce, shadeless heats of summer, caused many deaths. "Then was there a voice heard in Ramah, Rachel mourning for her children refused to be comforted because they were not." Much as it has improved of late years in salubrity, I am far from sure that Utah is yet a very healthy land for children. But as far as my experience goes, I think they are very kindly, as well as carefully nurtured. They are admitted very freely to their parents' society, and are not always "snubbed" when they proffer their small contributions to the conversation going on among their elders. Generally, too, they are well-behaved. I think the tie between mother and children is closer than that between them and the father. Whether the fathers can love each one of so many children, as much as they could if there were six or seven—or *say fifteen*—less, I will not pretend to say.

I have seen a Mormon father pet and humor a spoiled *thirty-fifth* child (a red-headed one, too!) with as unreasonable fondness as the youngest papa could show his first-born.

Two of the children my hostess at Fillmore had lost were twin girls, and she lamented over "Ada and Ida" quite as much as if they might not have grown up to be thirteenth or fourteenth wives to somebody. It had been one of the accepted beliefs with which my mind was stocked before entering Utah, that every mother would be found to regret the birth of a daughter as a misfortune. This is not so. They honestly believe in the grand calling their theology assigns to women; "that of endowing souls with tabernacles that they may accept redemption." Nowhere is the "sphere" of women, according to the gospel of Sarah Ellis, more fully recognized than in Utah; nowhere her "mission," according to Susan Anthony, more abhorred.

And yet they vote? True; but they do not take more interest in general politics than you do. If your husband, Charlotte, your father, brothers, and all the clergymen you know, approved of your voting, it would not strike you as an unfeminine proceeding. And if the matter on which your vote was required was one which might decide the question whether you were your husband's wife, and your children legitimate, you would be apt to entertain a determined opinion on the subject.

Nobody thought us unfeminine for being absorbingly interested in our national affairs during the war. The Utah women take a similar interest in the business of the world outside that concerns *them*; and pray over congressional debates as we prayed for our armies. (75–78)

When we reached the end of a day's journey, after taking off our outer garments and washing off the dust, it was the custom of our party to assemble before the fire in the sitting-room, and the leading "brothers and sisters" of the settlement would come in to pay their respects. The front door generally opened directly from the piazza into the parlor, and was always on the latch, and the circle round the fire varied constantly as the neighbors dropped in or went away. At these informal audiences, reports, complaints, and petitions were made; and I think I gathered more of the actual working of Mormonism by listening to them than from any other source. They talked away to Brigham Young about every conceivable matter, from the fluxing of an ore to the advantages of a Navajo bit, and expected him to remember every child in every cotter's family. And he really seemed to do so, and to be at home, and be rightfully deemed infallible on every subject. I think he must make fewer mistakes than most popes, from his being in such constant intercourse with his people. I noticed that he never seemed uninterested, but gave an unforced attention to the person addressing him, which suggested a mind free from care. I used to fancy that he wasted a great deal of power in this way; but I soon saw that he was accumulating it. Power, I mean, at least as the driving-wheel of his people's industry. (113–14)

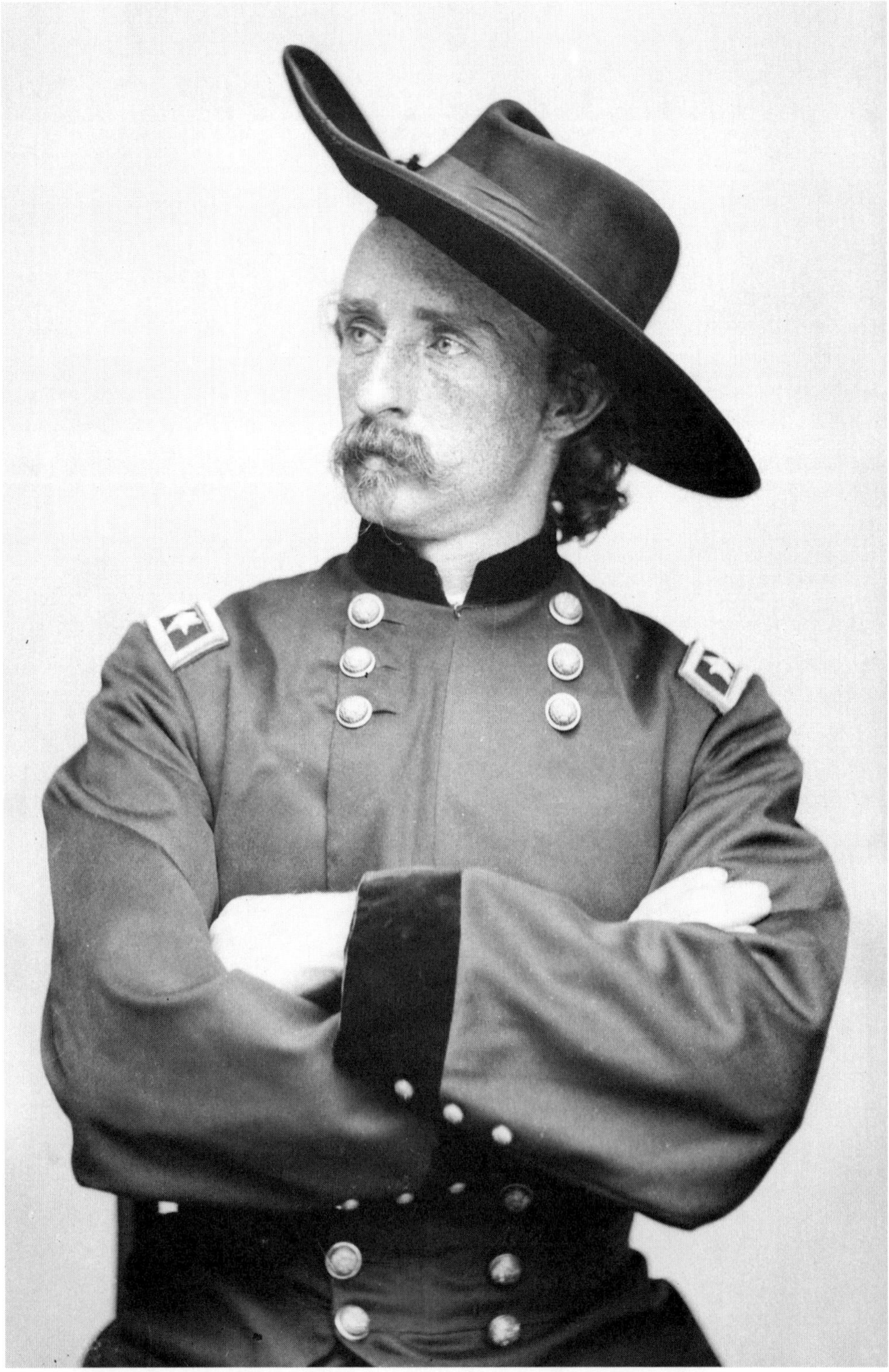

General George A. Custer

1875

General George A. Custer was the youngest general in the Union Army and fought at the first battle of Bull Run and at Gettysburg, among others. But he is remembered more for his campaigns against Native Americans in the West following the Civil War. Custer and his entire regiment were killed by Sioux Indians in South Dakota when he decided to attack before realizing that the Sioux greatly outnumbered his own men. General Custer gave the world the following explanation of why the Mormons got along with the Indians. Perhaps if he had followed the Mormon's example, he would have lived longer than he did.

> One reason is that they do not encroach on their territories as rapidly as we do. They do not require them to be constantly moving. They buy, and are slow to extend their boundaries. (Stanley P. Hirshson, *The Lion of the Lord*, 113)

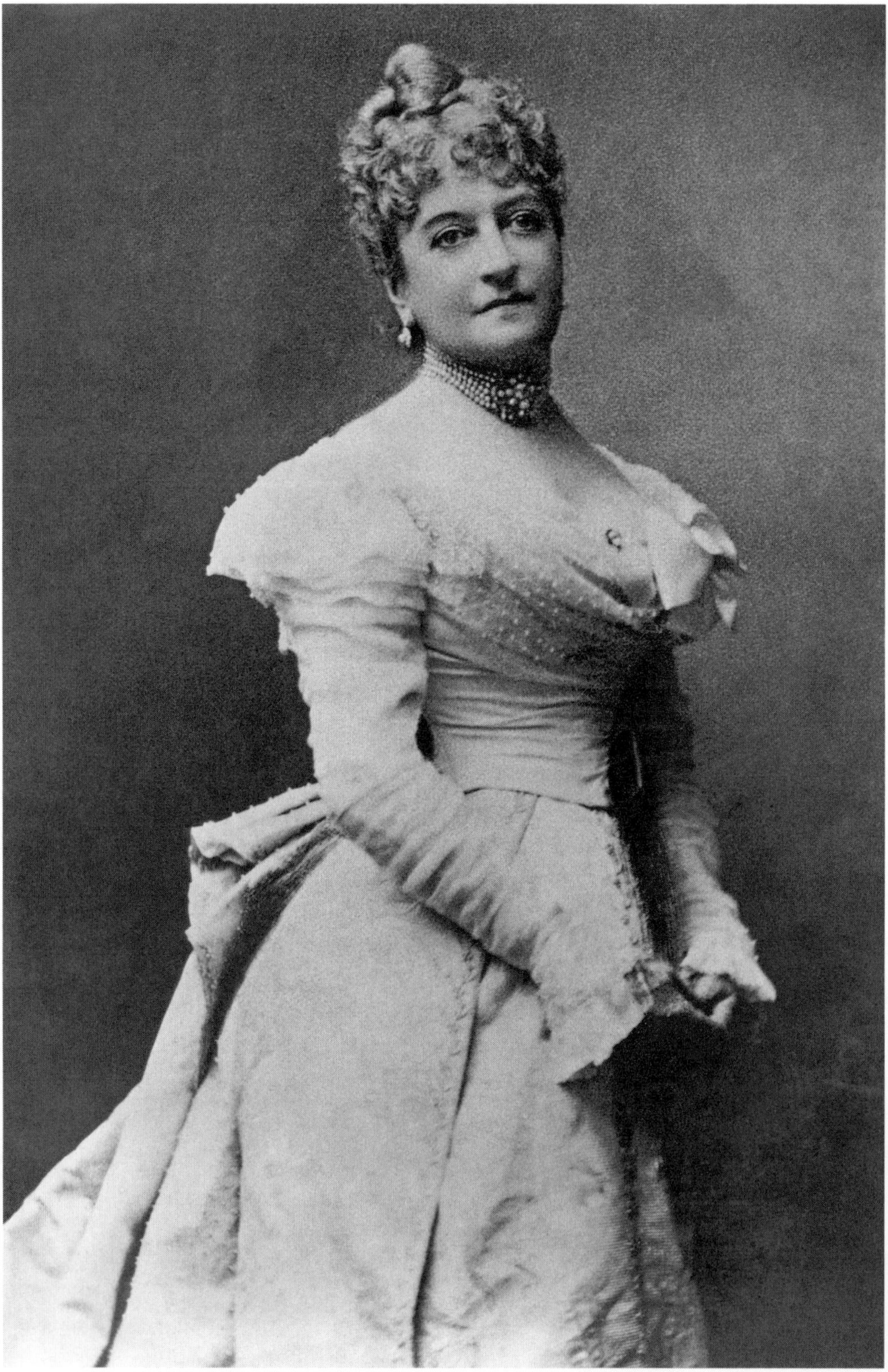

Miriam Florence Leslie

1877

Henry Carter, born in England in 1821, began his professional life as an engraver, using the pseudonym, Frank Leslie. In 1842 he decided to seek his fortune in the States, where he pioneered engraving techniques which allowed newspaper illustrations to be produced much faster than before. In 1855 he started Frank Leslie's Illustrated Newspaper, *and in 1857 he changed his name legally to Frank Leslie. He became a publishing giant, starting several popular magazines of the day. In 1874 he married Miriam Florence Folline, a descendant of French-Huguenot nobility. It was his second marriage, her third. From April to June, 1877, Miriam took a pleasure trip from New York to California, passing through Utah. When Frank died in 1880, his publishing empire was deeply in debt. But Miriam took over and soon made it prosper again. In 1882 she had her name changed legally to Frank Leslie. In 1891 she married Oscar Wilde's brother, William, but divorced him two years later. When she died in 1914 she willed her estate to women's suffrage. An interesting woman, she shared some interesting comments about Utah and the Mormons.*

We are in Utah, the land of thrift and industry, of agriculture and irrigation. We have been appalled by Nature in her unconquered might, in her resistless grandeur; we are now to admire her placidly yielding to man's dominion, and lending her creative forces to his guidance and direction.

The barren plains become verdant fields, the squalid cabin of the usual Western settler becomes a neat cottage, with flowers and garden-produce growing at its doors; the odious sage-brush disappears before the system of irrigation, which it dislikes as much as the more human indigenes of the prairies; men, women, and children are better fed, better dressed, and better mannered; in fact, as we stop in the first Mormon village, above whose single store are inscribed the mystic letters Z.C.M.I. (Zion's Co-operative Mercantile Institution), we feel

ZCMI dressed with a large U.S. flag for America's 200th birthday in 1979

a vague doubt and bewilderment stealing over our prejudices, not to say our principles, and are disposed to murmur, "Certainly, polygamy is very wrong, but roses are better than sage-brush, and potatoes and peas preferable as diet to buffalo grass. Also school-houses, with cleanly and comfortable troops of children about them, are a symptom of more advanced civilization than lonely shanties with only fever-and-ague and whisky therein. Why is nothing quite harmonious, quite consistent, quite perfect in this world?" and Echo Cañon echoes "Why?" (Mrs. Frank Leslie, *California: A Pleasure Trip*, 70–71)

The next morning we sallied forth to view the City of the Saints, with the same odd sort of excitement and vague expectation one must experience in Constantinople or Tangiers, or several other places which stand out in a traveler's memory as typical of a state of society utterly alien to his own. Nothing peculiar appeared at the outset, however, except that here for the first time did we perceive about the poorer houses that attempt at decoration, that consciousness that "a thing of beauty is a joy forever," which makes the difference between poverty and squalor; which shows that penury has neither broken the spirit nor crushed out the taste for refinement. Every house, however small or poor, had its little garden in front, filled with flowering shrubs or plants, many of them fruit trees, in this Spring time of the year rosy or white with bloom. Everywhere was thrift, care, the evidence of hard work, and a pride of ownership;

and oddly enough, these homes of rigid, yet tasteful and dignified poverty, reminded me of nothing so much as a Shaker village, visited not long since—a place where nobody was rich, nobody poor, nobody idle, nobody overworked, and where a certain prim love of the beautiful everywhere gilded the necessity of the useful. Is it that a strong religious conviction pervading a community, a religion that permeates every phase of life, has this effect upon outward forms of living? (74)

The editor of the Mormon paper proved a very intelligent and cultured man, and after a little talk he escorted us to see some of the lions of the place, first to the "Woman's Union," a large establishment, where the work of the women of Utah is collected and offered for sale. It is under the charge of a lady called Miss Snow [Eliza R.]—although she is one of Brigham Young's wives—two of his daughters, and Mrs. Davis. The large room on the ground floor was decorated with the American flag and three large mottoes done in white on a blue ground, to wit:

"Knowledge is Power."
"In Union is Strength."
"Success to Industry."

The goods consisted of every sort of home manufacture: clothes of all descriptions, shoes, bonnets, straw hats, artificial flowers, laces, including some beautiful wrought Honiton, and a piece of the first silk manufactured in Utah—a silver-gray fabric, resembling Japanese silk. Miss Snow presently entered, and greeted us pleasantly; she is a lady considerably past middle age, with a good and pleasing face, a quiet, refined manner, although cold and reserved, and a very precise and deliberate mode of speech. She seemed perfectly willing to talk upon any subject which we introduced, and quite able to give information in any direction indicated. She had been abroad, and told me she took cocoons of their own raising to Palestine, to compare with those of that country, and that the Utah article was pronounced fully equal to that of Oriental growth. She quietly acknowledged herself the principal mover in the Woman's Union, the object of which is to encourage self reliance, and perfect independence of the outside world, and added, with a smile of conscious strength and power: "We consider ourselves among the finest women in the world, and aim to compete with our sisters elsewhere in every pursuit and every branch of education." Women, she said, had as much interest as man in the prosperity of the territory, and their rights and privileges were equal. At the two colleges of Utah the course of study was the same for male and female students, and the progress of the latter was fully equal to the former. Education had necessarily been neglected among them in the first hard years of struggle, when every one had

> *We consider ourselves among the finest women in the world.*

to labor for the means of bare existence; but now good schools were established everywhere, and the rising generation would be admirably trained.

In this connection she spoke of the hard journey across the plains thirty years ago, when, on the twelfth of June, leaving the place where Omaha now stands, they did not arrive at Salt Lake until the second day of October.

We touched slightly upon the peculiar institution of Utah, and I inquired if the various wives of one husband got along amicably among themselves, to which she decisively replied: "Perfectly so, their religion inculcates it; and besides, their work is so large, and their aims so high, that they have no time and no capacity for petty jealousies."

While talking we turned over some of the books by Mormon authors for sale here, and noticed a volume of Voyages by Miss Snow, and also a collection of poems, but she herself was more interesting than her books, and seemed so strong and earnest, and full of ideas and aspirations, and plans for the widest good of her chosen people, that we left her with real regret. (77–80)

The finest building within many hundred miles, perhaps, is the Amelia Palace, a really magnificent house, nearly finished, and designed for the wife whom our photographer sternly denies to be the favorite, and whose name it bears. It is really a splendid edifice. (95)

We will speak of its present apostle, President (of the Church) Young, whom we found standing in the middle of his Office to receive us, with an expression of weary fortitude upon his face, and a perfunctoriness of manner, suggesting that parties of Eastern visitors, curiosity seekers, and interviewers might possibly have become a trifle tedious in Salt Lake City and the Office of the President.

"How do you do! glad to see you! pass on, if you please!" was the salutation, accompanied with a touch of the hand as each guest was presented and named and when nearly all had passed on and sat down, and the host resumed his own seat, an awful pause fell upon the assembled company, broken presently by a sonorous assertion from the President that it was a pleasant day. This was eagerly assented to by the Chief, who added that the weather had been fine for some days, and the conversation flowed on in this agreeable strain for some moments, during which time we studied the personal appearance of the lion we had come out for to see. We found it both formidable and attractive: a fine, tall well developed figure; a fresh, ready, ruddy complexion almost befitting a young girl; keen blue eyes, not telling too much of what goes on behind them; a full mouth; a singularly magnetic manner; a voice hard and cold in its formal speech, but low and impressive when used confidentially; altogether a man of mark anywhere, and one whose wonderful influence over the minds and purses of men, and the hearts and principles of women, can be much more fully credited after an hour's conversation than before.

Perceiving that the interview was but a "function" for President Young, and one of whose brevity would doubtless be the soul of its wit, we resolved to constitute ourselves the Curtius of our party, and, approaching the sacred sofa, remarked to the Chief, who was seated thereon, that we would change places with him as we had some information to ask of the President.

The Chief rose with suspicious alacrity, and for the first time a gleam of interest shone in Brigham's pale blue eyes as he turned them upon the bold intruder, whose first question was:

"Do you suppose, Mr. President, that I came all the way to Salt Lake City to hear that it was a fine day?"

"I am sure you need not, my dear," was the ready response of this cavalier of seventy-six years, "for it must be fine weather wherever you are!"

The conversation established after this method went upon velvet, and, as the rest of the party began to talk among themselves, presently assumed a confidential and interesting turn, and we felt that what Mr. Young said upon matters of Mormon faith and Mormon practice he said with a sincerity and earnestness not always felt in a man's more public and general utterances.

Glancing at Joseph Smith's picture, we ventured the criticism that it did not show any great amount of strength, intelligence, or culture. Mr. Young admitted the criticism, and said that Smith was not a man of great character naturally, but that he was inspired by God as a prophet, and spoke at times not from himself but by inspiration; he was not a man of education, but received such enlightenment from the Holy Spirit that he needed nothing more to fit him for his work as a leader. "And this is my own case also," pursued Mr. Young, quite simply. "My father was a frontiersman, unlearned, and obliged to struggle for his children's food day by day, with no time to think of their education. All that I have acquired is by my own exertions and by the grace of God, who sometimes chooses the weak things of earth to manifest His glory." This want of education, he went on to say, was one of the greatest drawbacks and trials to the older generation of Mormons; they had been, almost without exception, poor and unlettered people, gathered from all parts of the world, and obliged, especially after their arrival in Utah, to use every energy and all their time to make productive and life-sustaining homes from the desert lands and savage wilderness into which they had penetrated; since, only thus shut off from other men could they hope to enjoy their religion and practices unmolested.

"But all this is over now, thank God!" ejaculated the President, with a gesture of relief. "Our homes are made, our country is prosperous, and our educational privileges are equal or superior to any State in the Union. Every child six years of age in the territory can read and write, and there is no limit to what they may learn as they grow older."

> *He was inspired by God as a prophet, and spoke at times not from himself but by inspiration.*

※

We spoke of the magnificence of the Amelia Palace, and he characterized it as "absurdly fine"; but when we suggested that nothing could be too much for so good a wife and so lovely a woman as she was said to be, he assented, and added, emphatically, "She is all that, and more. Yes, Amelia is a good wife, an excellent wife and a lovely woman," with other phrases expressive of tenderness and esteem. "Besides," added the writer, "the Beehive, which is, I believe, your present residence, looks to me rather shabby for a man of your position;" but at this he shook his head, saying: "There it is, there it is; extravagance and ambition come creeping in, and destroy the simplicity of the first ideas. The Beehive was good enough for me, and has been so for many a year, but the world is changing—changing!" (96–100)

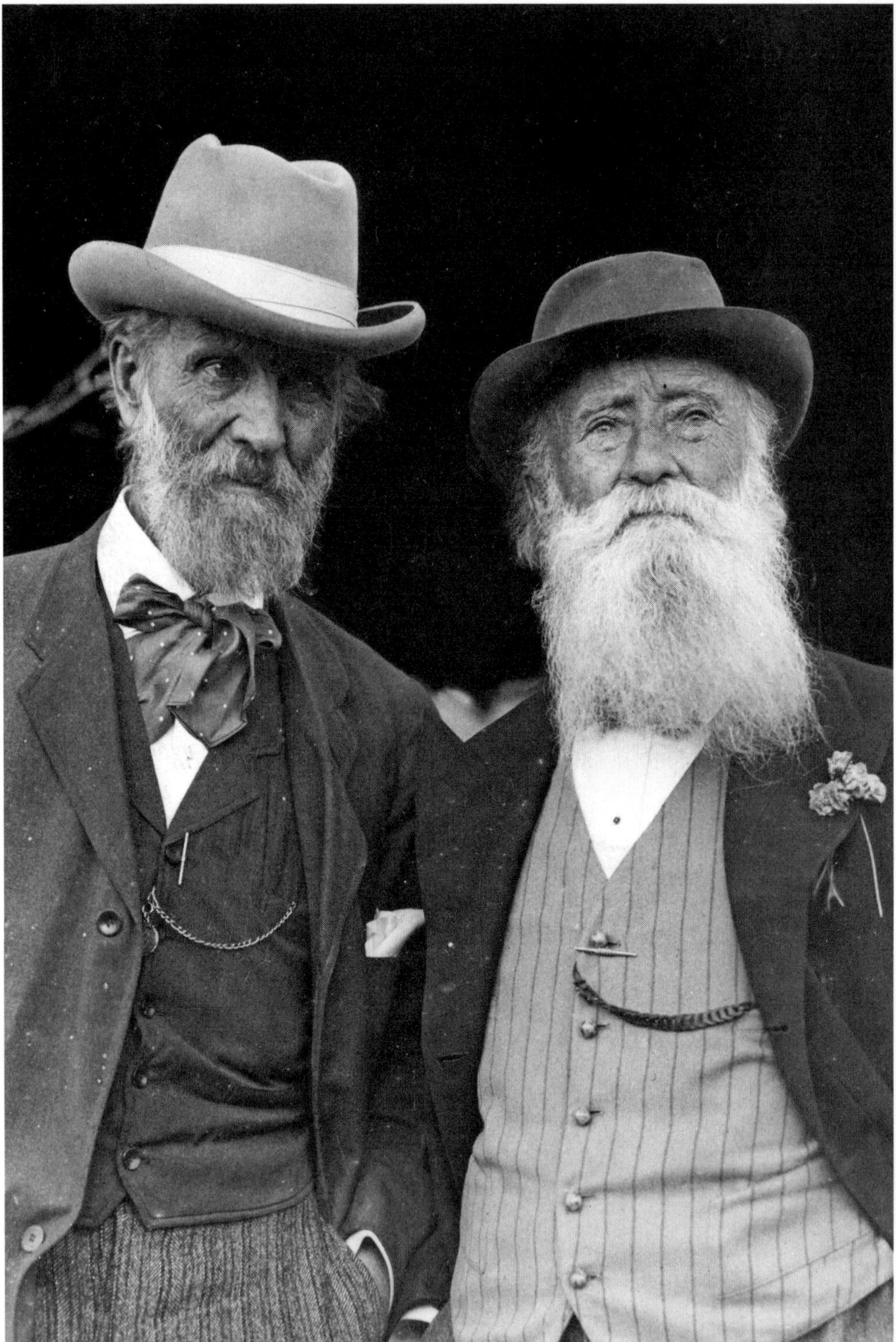

John Muir

1877

Most people were drawn to Utah because of the unique people. When John Muir, a naturalist who advocated conservation and national parks, arrived in May, 1877, however, he was more interested in Utah's natural attractions. Even when he describes people and buildings, he presents them in their relationship with nature.

The mountains rise grandly round about this curious city, the Zion of the new Saints, so grandly that the city itself is hardly visible. The Wahsatch [sic] Range, snow-laden and adorned with glacier-sculptured peaks, stretches continuously along the eastern horizon, forming the boundary of the Great Salt Lake Basin; while across the valley of the Jordan south-westward from here, you behold the Oquirrh Range, about as snowy and lofty as the Wahsatch. To the northwest your eye skims the blue levels of the great lake, out of the midst of which rise island mountains, and beyond, at a distance of fifty miles, is seen the picturesque wall of the lakeside mountains blending with the lake and the sky.

The glacial developments of these superb ranges are sharply sculptured peaks and crests, with ample wombs between them where the ancient snows of the glacial period were collected and transformed into ice, and ranks of profound shadowy cañons, while moraines commensurate with the lofty fountains extend into the valleys, forming far the grandest series of glacial monuments I have yet seen this side of the Sierra.

In beginning this letter I meant to describe the city, but in the company of these noble old mountains, it is not easy to bend one's attention upon anything else. Salt Lake cannot be called a very beautiful town, neither is there anything ugly or repulsive about it. From the slopes of the Wahsatch foothills,

John Muir, naturalist in his element, in 1902

or old lake benches, toward Fort Douglas it is seen to occupy the sloping gravelly delta of City Creek, a fine, hearty stream that comes pouring from the snows of the mountains through a majestic glacial cañon; and it is just where this stream comes forth into the light on the edge of the valley of the Jordan that the Mormons have built their new Jerusalem

At first sight there is nothing very marked in the external appearance of the town excepting its leafiness. Most of the houses are veiled with trees, as if set down in the midst of one grand orchard; and seen at a little distance they appear like a field of glacier boulders overgrown with aspens, such as one often meets in the upper valleys of the California Sierra, for only the angular roofs are clearly visible.

Perhaps nineteen twentieths of the houses are built of bluish-gray adobe bricks, and are only one or two stories high, forming fine cottage homes which promise simple comfort within. They are set well back from the street, leaving room for a flower garden, while almost every one has a thrifty orchard at the sides and around the back. The gardens are laid out with great simplicity, indicating love for flowers by people comparatively poor, rather than deliberate efforts of the rich for showy artistic effects. They are like the pet gardens of children, about as artless and humble, and harmonize with the low dwellings to which they belong. In almost every one you find daisies, and mint, and lilac bushes, and rows of plain English tulips. Lilacs and tulips are the most characteristic flowers, and nowhere have I seen them in greater perfection. As Oakland is preëminently a city of roses, so is this Mormon Saints' Rest a city of lilacs and tulips. The flowers, at least, are saintly, and they are surely loved. Scarce a home, however obscure, is without them, and the simple, unostentatious manner in which they are planted and gathered in pots and boxes about the windows shows how truly they are prized.

The surrounding commons, the marshy levels of the Jordan, and dry, gravelly lake benches on the slopes of the Wahsatch foothills are now gay with wild flowers, chief among which are a species of phlox, with an abundance of rich pink corollas, growing among sagebrush in showy tufts, and a beautiful papilionaceous plant, with silky leaves and large clusters of purple flowers, banner, wings, and keel exquisitely shaded, a mertensia, hydrophyllum, white boragewort, orthocarpus, several species of violets, and a tall scarlet gilia. It is delightful to see how eagerly all these are sought after by the children, both boys and girls. Every day that I have gone botanizing I have met groups of little Latter-Days with their precious bouquets, and at such times it was hard to believe the dark, bloody passages of Mormon history.

But to return to the city. As soon as City Creek approaches its upper limit its waters are drawn off right and left, and distributed in brisk rills, one on each side of every street, the regular slopes of the delta upon which the city is built being admirably adapted to this system of street irrigation. These streams are all pure and sparkling in the upper streets, but, as they are used to some extent as sewers, they soon manifest the consequences of contact with civilization, though the speed of their flow prevents their becoming offensive, and little Saints not over particular may be seen drinking from them everywhere.

The streets are remarkably wide and the buildings low, making them appear yet wider than they really are. Trees are planted along the sidewalks—elms, poplars, maples, and a few catalpas and hawthorns; yet they are mostly small and irregular, and nowhere form avenues half so leafy and imposing as one would be led to expect. Even in the business streets there is but little regularity in the buildings—now a row of plain adobe structures, half store, half dwelling, then a high mercantile block of red brick or sandstone, and again a row of adobe cottages nestled back among apple trees. There is one immense store with its sign upon the roof, in letters big enough to be read miles away, "Z.C.M.I." (Zion's Cooperative Mercantile Institution), while many a small, codfishy corner grocery bears the legend "Holiness to the Lord, Z.C.M.I." But little evidence will you find in this Zion, with its fifteen thousand souls, of great wealth, though many a Saint is seeking it as keenly as any Yankee Gentile. But on the other hand, searching throughout all the city, you will not find any trace of squalor or extreme poverty. (John Muir, *Steep Trails*, 105–9)

> *Throughout all the city, you will not find any trace of squalor or extreme poverty.*

Lady Mary Duffus Hardy

1880

Lady Mary McDowell Duffus Hardy was one of many aristocrats who decided that Utah and the Mormons were a must for any exotic adventurer. On her journey through the states she spent several days in Ogden and Salt Lake.

[T]here are few passengers on board the train as we steam through the suburban districts of Mormonland. The magnificent chain of the Wahsatch [sic] Mountains rising in the east, and the great Salt Lake stretching away toward the west, the rest of the scene made up of fertile lands, green meadows, fields of yellow corn, and purple clover, form an enchanting panorama as we fly past them; we are full of an undefined curiosity and anxious to see this City of the Saints of which we have heard so much. We soon discover that none but the "Saints" are employed on board this train, none but Mormon faces gather round us, they check our baggage, punch our tickets, and render us every necessary courtesy, which would do credit to the gentlest of Gentiles. Our conductor seems disposed to make himself quite at home; he takes a seat beside us, and commences a pleasant conversation; he knows we are from England, and proceeds to give us all kinds of miscellaneous and useful information. He points out the different features in the landscape, and tells us of thrifty villages and thriving farms which are scattered among the mountains. He talks freely of the flourishing condition of the City of the Saints: but he avoids any special allusion to the peculiarities of the saints themselves. During our two hours' run from Ogden to Salt Lake city he grows more and more sociably disposed. We try to guide the conversation into the channel where we desire it should go. We wonder whether he is a Mormon or one of the Gentile sect, which is now numerously represented in that once exclusive land. We ask the question pointblank.

"Yes, ma'am, I'm proud to say I am," he answers, swelling with invisible glory; it is now he informs us that the whole line of railway was built by the Mormon people, and is exclusively run by them, no other labour being employed.

"I came here," he adds, "when I was six years old, when our people were forced to leave Nauvoo. I remember trotting along by my mother's side as we were driven out of the city at the point of the bayonet, the soldiers pricking and goading us like cattle. I shall never forget that time,—never, if I live to be a hundred years old; but we pulled through, and here we are in the most beautiful and flourishing valley in the whole wide world." . . .

Here we are in the most beautiful and flourishing valley in the whole wide world.

We reach the City of the Saints at last, and find it as fair and beautiful as we had expected. It is in truth an oasis in a desert, a blooming garden in a wilderness of green. We can scarcely conceive how this flowery world has lifted itself from the heart of desolation; it is only one more proof that the intellect and industry of man can master the mysteries of nature, and force her in her most harsh uncompromising moods to bring forth fair fruits. It lies in a deep wide valley, bounded on the east by the mighty range of the Wahsatch Mountains, which lift their lonely ice-crowned heads far into the skies, their rugged stony feet stretching away and reaching towards the west, where the great Salt Lake unrolls its dark waters, and widens and wanders away until it is lost in the distance. The streets are wide, the houses of all sorts and sizes, some one storey high, some two or even three, all built in different styles, or no style of architecture; each man having built his dwelling in accordance with his own taste or convenience. The streets are all arranged in long straight rows, and stretch away till they seem to crawl up the mountain-sides and then are lost. On either side of the roadways are magnificent forest-trees, which in summer-time must form a most delightful shade, though now it is autumn and the leaves are falling fast. Streams of water with their pleasant gurgling music flow on either side, through a deep cutting (which we should irreverently call the gutter), rushing along as though they were in a hurry to reach some everlasting sea. The women come out with their buckets and help themselves, while the children sail their toy boats, clapping their hands gleefully as the tiny craft is tossed, and tumbled, and borne along on the face of the bubbling water. Streetcars come crawling along the straight streets, crossing and recrossing each other at different points; but a private cab or carriage is rarely to be seen. Every house, be it only composed of a single room, is surrounded by a plot of garden ground, where fruits, flowers, and vegetables all grow together in loving companionship. Everything seems flourishing, and everybody seems well-to-do; there are no signs of poverty anywhere; no bare-footed whining beggars fill the streets; tramps there may be, passing from one part of the State to another, but these are all decently dressed and well fed, for at whatever door they knock they are sure to find food and shelter, charity to those in need being a part of the reigning religion.

The children who swarm on all sides are the healthiest, rosiest, happiest looking urchins conceivable; some perfectly beautiful specimens of young humanity. One felt sorry to think they must develop into the bewhiskered man or befrizzled woman; there was not a pale or sickly face in all the multitude. There are no signs of rank or fashion anywhere; there are no drones lounging about in this community, they are all busy bees; every man and every woman, too, does his or her share in the labour market, all according to their special abilities; and here is the only true republic in all America, elsewhere it is the name and not the thing. Here republicanism exists in its genuine form; it is not a commune, and encourages no communistic principles. Here every one must work, uniting therein for the common good of all. Wealth, represented by gold or other possessions, is unequally distributed as in other large cities. Some live in large houses, some in small, some wear broadcloth, some wear frieze; but the man who labours with his hands and the man who works with his brain, those who plan and those who execute, live together in a common brotherhood—for they are equally well educated, and have grown up in or helped to make the world they live in. The idle or the dissolute are speedily hunted out of the community. There is an equality in tone and manner among all conditions of people which strikes rather discordantly upon our ideas of the harmony of things, but we soon get used to it. We meet with a general pleasant courtesy, which is never vulgar, never over-free; there is a sense of equality, a sort of "one man as good as another," which is always felt though never obtrusively asserted. The woman who washes your linen, and the man who wheels your baggage, do it with a sort of courteous friendliness, considering that you are as much obliged to them as they to you; no kind of manual labour is looked upon as discreditable or below the dignity of any man. I have seen a Mormon bishop, in his shirt sleeves and corduroys, working hard in a timber-yard or carpentering at a bench. Schools and churches of all denominations and creeds abound; every child has a right to an equal education at the expense of the State of Utah. . . . Signs of prosperity and plenty are everywhere; to the mere passer-by or transient traveller, who can judge from out-

> *The State of Utah is the most flourishing in the Union.*

ward appearances only, the State of Utah is the most flourishing in the Union. With its mines, its metals, its marvellous agricultural productions, its wealth of fruits and flowers, it seems as though the horn of plenty emptied itself in the lap of this favoured land. Out of doors in the streets the brisk, bustling population are crowding to and fro, all is gay and bright; the sun shines, the genial air stirs and invigorates the spirit, the pulse beats to healthful music, while the surrounding scene of swelling hills and glorious mountains is beautiful to behold. (Lady Mary Duffus Hardy, *Through Cities and Prarie Lands*, 102–7)

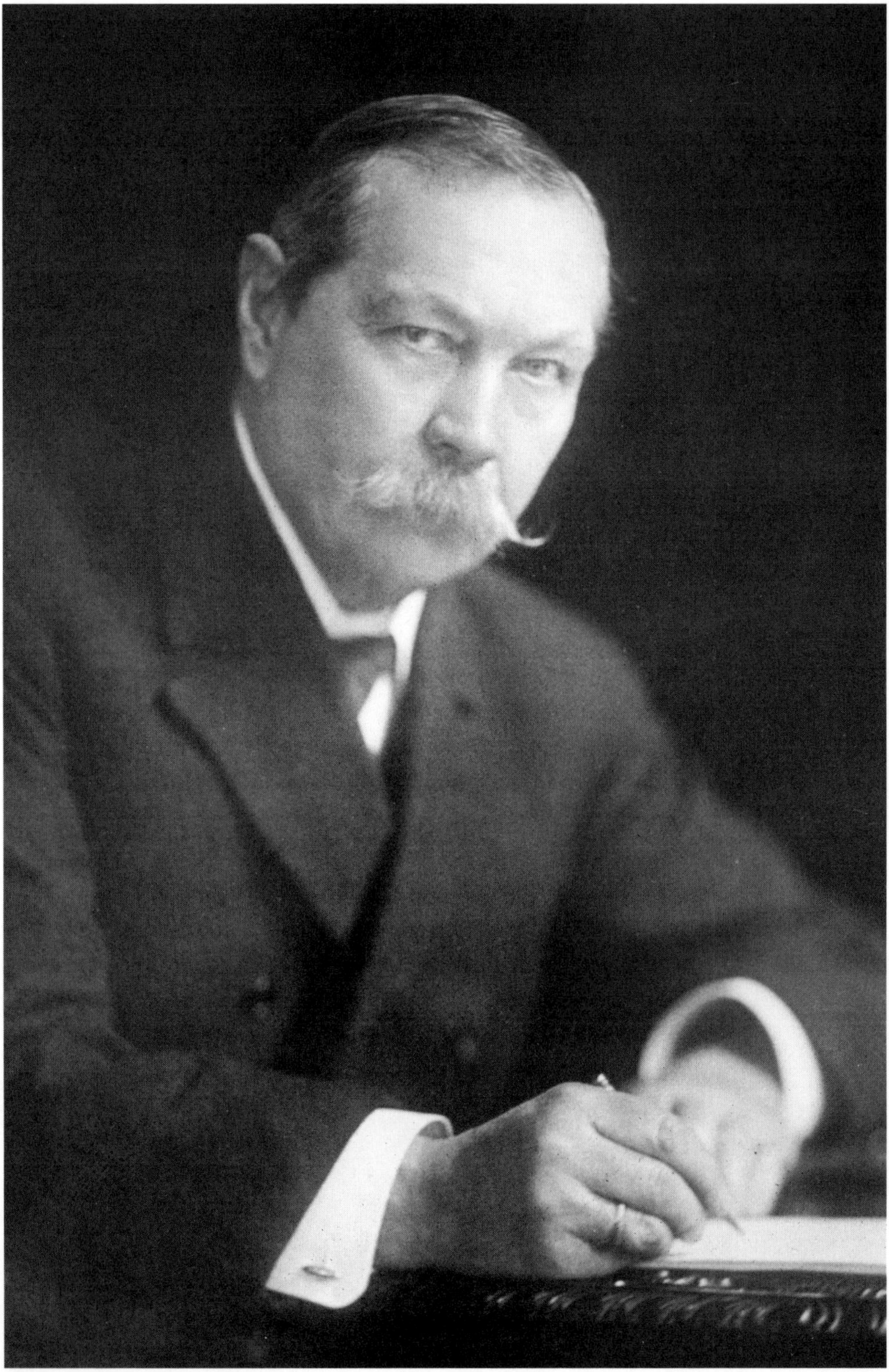

Sir Arthur Conan Doyle
1887

Did you know that the Mormons helped launch Sherlock Holmes? A Study In Scarlet, *a tale of Danites and murder, was the first Holmes-solved case that British author Sir Arthur Conan Doyle published. Doyle earned a medical degree but gave up practicing medicine to write full-time three years after* A Study in Scarlet *was published. The Sherlock Holmes novels were popular and are still famous today for the way Holmes uses logical reasoning to solve complex cases. However, it's clear from the first Sherlock Holmes story that Doyle was not as careful in his research as he expected his famous detective to be.*

One fine morning John Ferrier was about to set out to his wheat-fields, when he heard the click of the latch, and, looking through the window, saw a stout, sandy-haired, middle-aged man coming up the pathway. His heart leapt to his mouth, for this was none other than the great Brigham Young himself. Full of trepidation—for he knew that such a visit boded him little good—Ferrier ran to the door to greet the Mormon chief. The latter, however, received his salutations coldly, and followed him with a stern face into the sitting-room.

"Brother Ferrier," he said, taking a seat, and eying the farmer keenly from under his light-colored eyelashes, "the true believers have been good friends to you. We picked you up when you were starving in the desert, we shared our food with you, led you safe to the Chosen Valley, gave you a goodly share of land, and allowed you to wax rich under our protection. Is not this so?"

"It is so," answered John Ferrier.

"In return for all this we asked but one condition: that was, that you should embrace the true faith, and conform in every way to its usages. This you promised to do, and this, if common report says truly, you have neglected."

"And how have I neglected it?" asked Ferrier, throwing out his hands in expostulation. "Have I not given to the common fund? Have I not attended at the temple? Have I not—?"

"Where are your wives?" asked Young, looking round him. "Call them in that I may greet them."

"It is true that I have not married," Ferrier answered. "But women were few, and there were many who had better claims than I. I was not a lonely man: I had my daughter to attend to my wants."

"It is of that daughter that I would speak to you," said the leader of the Mormons. "She has grown to be the flower of Utah, and has found favor in the eyes of many who are high in the land."

John Ferrier groaned internally.

"There are stories of her which I would fain disbelieve—stories that she is sealed to some Gentile. This must be the gossip of idle tongues. What is the thirteenth rule in the code of the sainted Joseph Smith? 'Let every maiden of the true faith marry one of the elect; for if she wed a Gentile, she commits a grievous sin.' This being so, it is impossible that you, who profess the holy creed, should suffer your daughter to violate it."

John Ferrier made no answer, but he played nervously with his riding-whip.

"Upon this one point your whole faith shall be tested—so it has been decided in the Sacred Council of Four. The girl is young, and we would not have her wed gray hairs, neither would we deprive her all choice. We Elders have many heifers, but our children must also be provided. Stangerson has a son and Drebber has a son, and either of them would gladly welcome your daughter to his house. Let her choose between them. They are young and rich and of the true faith. What say you to that?"

Ferrier remained silent for some little time, with his brows knitted.

"You will give us time," he said, at last. "My daughter is very young—she is scarce of an age to marry."

"She shall have a month to choose," said Young, rising from his seat. "At the end of that time she shall give her answer."

He was passing through the door, when he turned, with flushed face and flashing eyes. "It were better for you, John Ferrier," he thundered, "that you and she were now lying blanched

Sir Arthur Conan Doyle, creator of Sherlock Holmes

skeletons upon the Sierra Blanco, than that you should put your weak wills against the orders of the Holy Four!"

With a threatening gesture of his hand, he turned from the door, and Ferrier heard his heavy steps scrunching along the shingly path. (Sir Arthur Conan Doyle, *A Study in Scarlet,* 101–3)

Doyle visited Utah and spoke in the Tabernacle in 1923

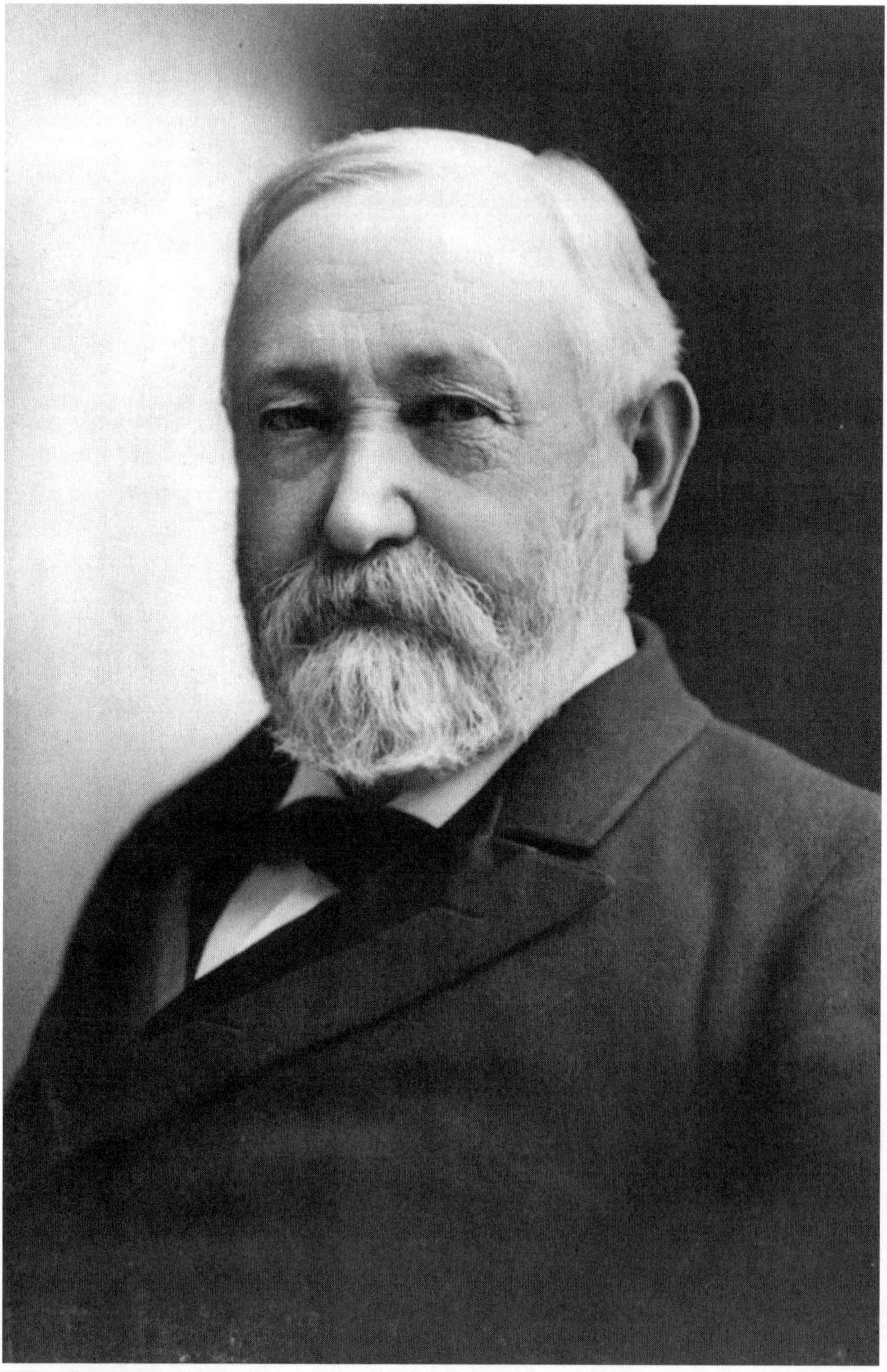

Benjamin Harrison

1891

President Benjamin Harrison didn't like what he had heard about Mormons' practice of polygamy and feared that the 1890 Manifesto wasn't sincere—that the citizens of Utah were lying in their pledge to cease practicing polygamy so that Utah could become a state. After President Harrison saw Utah for himself, his heart softened toward Mormons.

"I have not seen in all this long journey," the president said, "anything that touched my heart more than . . . when the children from the free public schools of Salt Lake City, waving the one banner that we all love and singing an anthem of praise to that beneficent Providence . . . , gave us their glad welcome. . . . I have seen nothing more beautiful and inspiring than this scene which burst upon us unexpectedly. The multitude of children bearing waving banners makes a scene which can never fade from our memories. . . .

"It has been very pleasant to-day to ride through this most extraordinary valley [Utah County] and to notice how productive your fields are an how genial and kindly your people are." (*Presidents and Prophets*, 171–72)

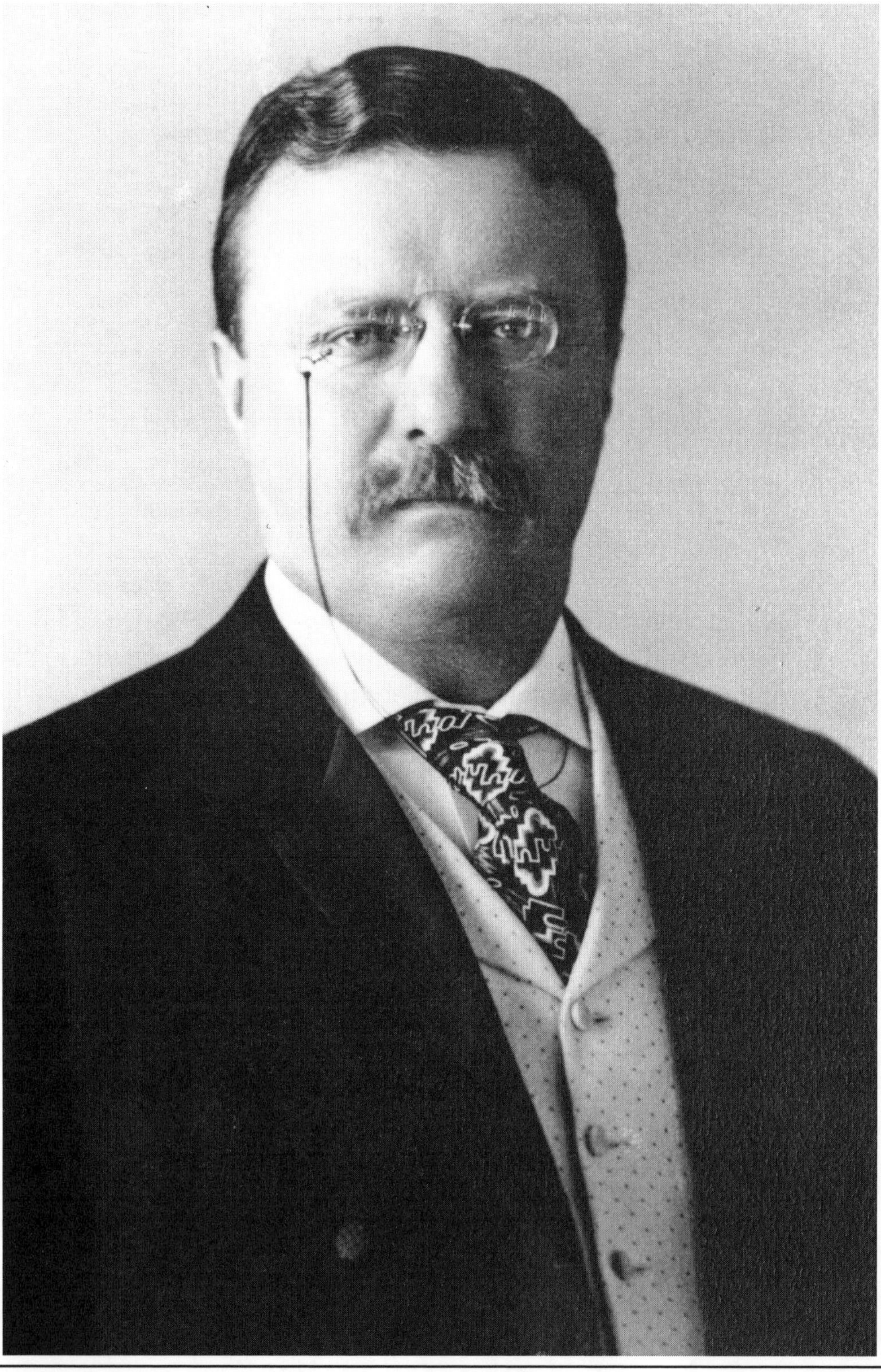

President Theodore Roosevelt

1911

President Theodore Roosevelt is often remembered for his enthusiasm and energy—as well as his forcefulness. He did not talk softly, but he did wield a big stick in defending Utah's Senator Reed Smoot* from charges of being a polygamist. He also defended himself from those who accused him of making a deal with the Mormons to decrease federal pressure on them in exchange for the electoral votes of Utah, Wyoming, and Idaho.

I have known monogamous "Mormons" whose standard of domestic life and morality and whose attitude toward the relations of men and women was as high as that of the best citizens of any other creed; indeed, among these "Mormons" the standard of sexual morality was unusually high. Their children were numerous, healthy, and well brought up; their young men were less apt than their neighbors to indulge in that course of vicious sexual dissipation so degrading to manhood and so brutal in the degradation it inflicts on women; and they were free from that vice, more destructive to civilization than any other can possibly be, the artificial restriction of families, the practice of sterile marriage; and which ultimately means destruction of the nation. The loss of the paternal and maternal instincts among men and women, the deification of a cold, calculating selfishness, the failure to understand that there are no other joys and no other duties as great as the joys and the duties connected with the happy family life of father, mother, and children—all this represents a far worse evil than even the worst of purely political evils can be. The evil of divorce and all kindred evils are merely subsidiary in wickedness and evil results to this

During his first visit to Utah, New York governor and vice presidential candidate Theodore Roosevelt (far left) visits Saltair resort at the Great Salt Lake in September 1900 with Utah's first governor, Heber M. Wells (in the top hat center)

great and central evil. If the average man is not most anxious to be a good father, performing his full duty to his wife and children; if the average woman is not most anxious to be a good and happy wife and mother, the mother of plenty of healthy and happy and well-trained children; then not only have the average man and the average woman missed what is infinitely the highest happiness of life, but they are bad citizens of the worst type; and the nation in which they represent the average type of citizen is doomed to undergo the hopeless disaster which it deserves. In so far as the "Mormons" will stand against all hideous and degrading tendencies of this kind, they will set a good example of citizenship. (*Improvement Era,* 718)

* Reed Smoot was an Apostle at the time of his election in 1902, and for four years he battled the Senate for the right to take his appointed seat. The Senate didn't want to allow Smoot to serve because of his Apostle status and the Church's policy regarding plural marriage. Finally, in 1907, Smoot was seated and continued to serve as a Utah senator until 1933.

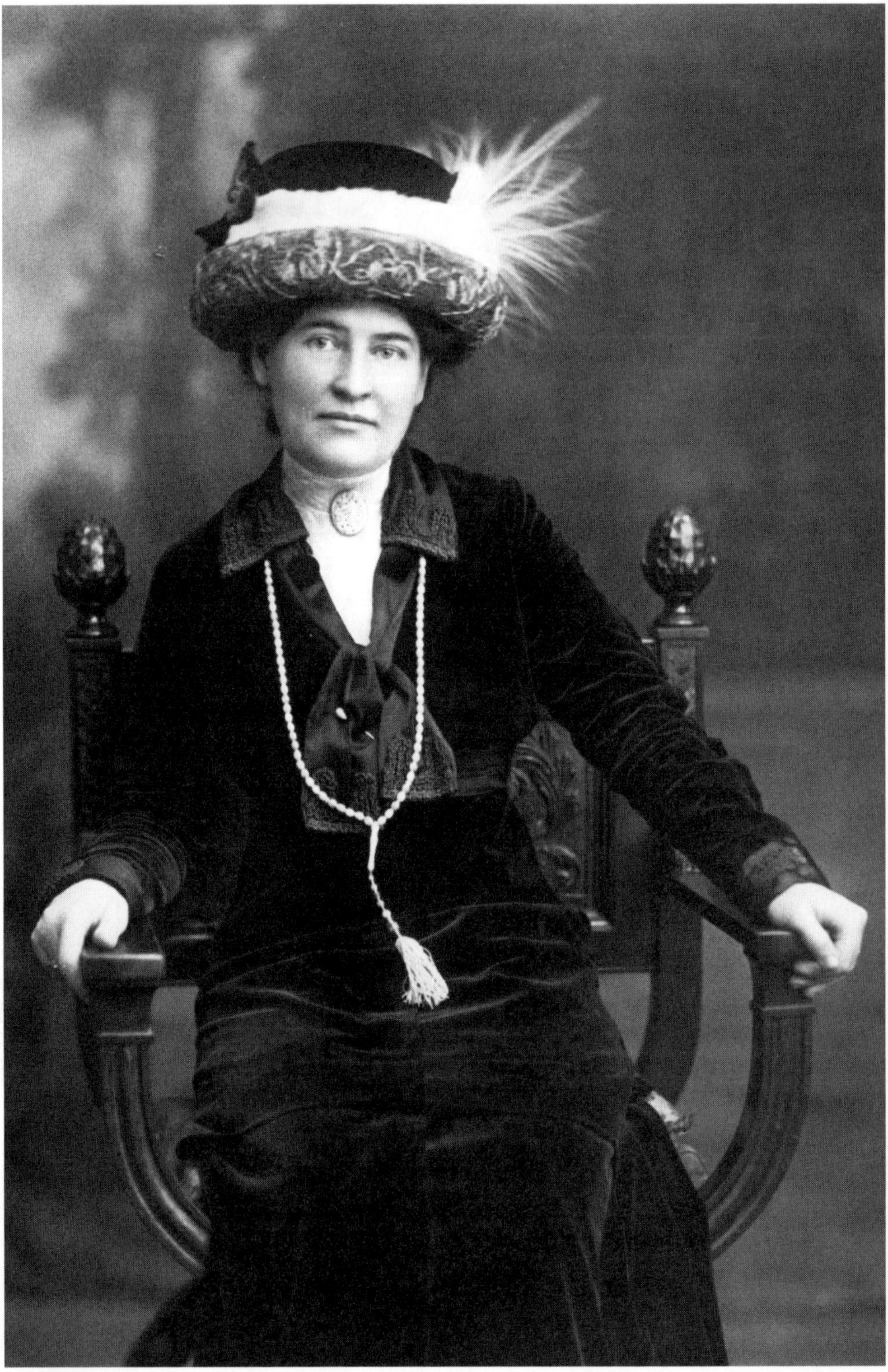

WILLA CATHER
1918

Celebrated American novelist Willa Cather spent some of her childhood on the Nebraska frontier. She graduated from the University of Nebraska before moving to New York and pursuing a career in magazine editing and creative writing. Her works celebrate the spirit of the American West and the courage of pioneers—even Mormon pioneers.

All the years that have passed have not dimmed my memory of that first glorious autumn. The new country lay open before me: there were no fences in those days, and I could choose my own way over the grass uplands, trusting the pony to get me home again. Sometimes I followed the sunflower-bordered roads. Fuchs told me that the sunflowers were introduced into that country by the Mormons; that at the time of the persecution, when they left Missouri and struck out into the wilderness to find a place where they could worship God in their own way, the members of the first exploring party, crossing the plains to Utah, scattered sunflower seed as they went. The next summer, when the long trains of wagons

Author Willa Cather at the height of her career

came through with all the women and children, they had the sunflower trail to follow. I believe that botanists do not confirm Fuchs's story, but insist that the sunflower was native to those plains. Nevertheless, that legend has stuck in my mind, and sunflower-bordered roads always seem to me the roads to freedom. (Willa Cather, *My Ántonia*, 28–29)

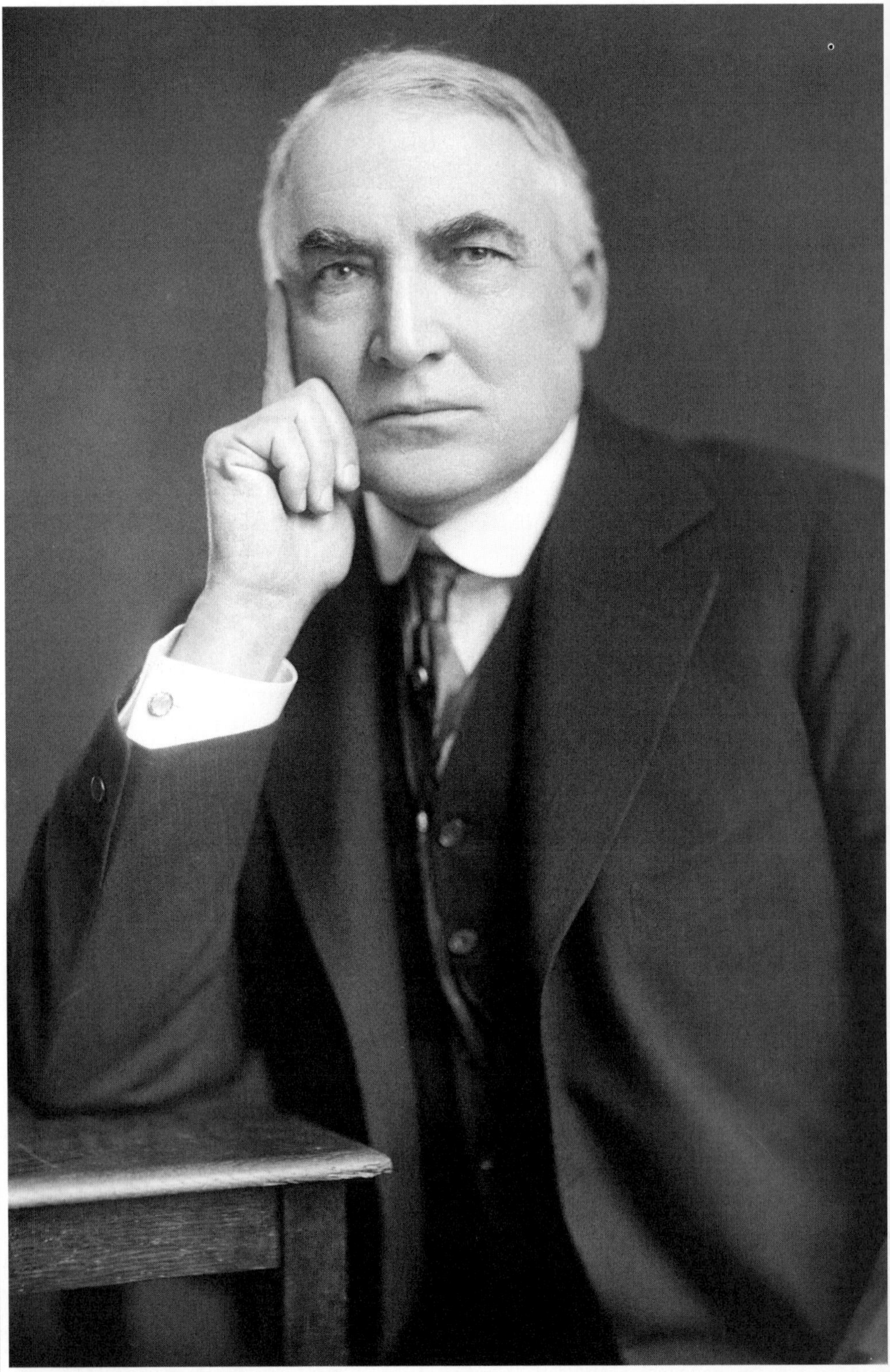

President Warren G. Harding

1923

President Warren G. Harding was a friend of LDS Apostle-Senator Reed Smoot. Elder Smoot gave President Harding a Book of Mormon, discussed the gospel with him, and even gave the president's wife a priesthood blessing when she was ill. Smoot found Harding to be respectful and receptive to Mormon beliefs.

> I do not know but what Brigham Young was right in his religion. . . .
>
> I have found a new slogan in your wonderful country, which I am delighted to adopt, namely, the one which refers to 'Utah's best crop.' I do not know when I have seen so many happy, smiling, sturdy children in so short a period of travel. A thousand delights have come to us in getting more intimately acquainted with your wonderful country . . . but I love, above all else, the boyhood and girlhood of marvelous Utah. (*Presidents and Prophets,* 220, 221)

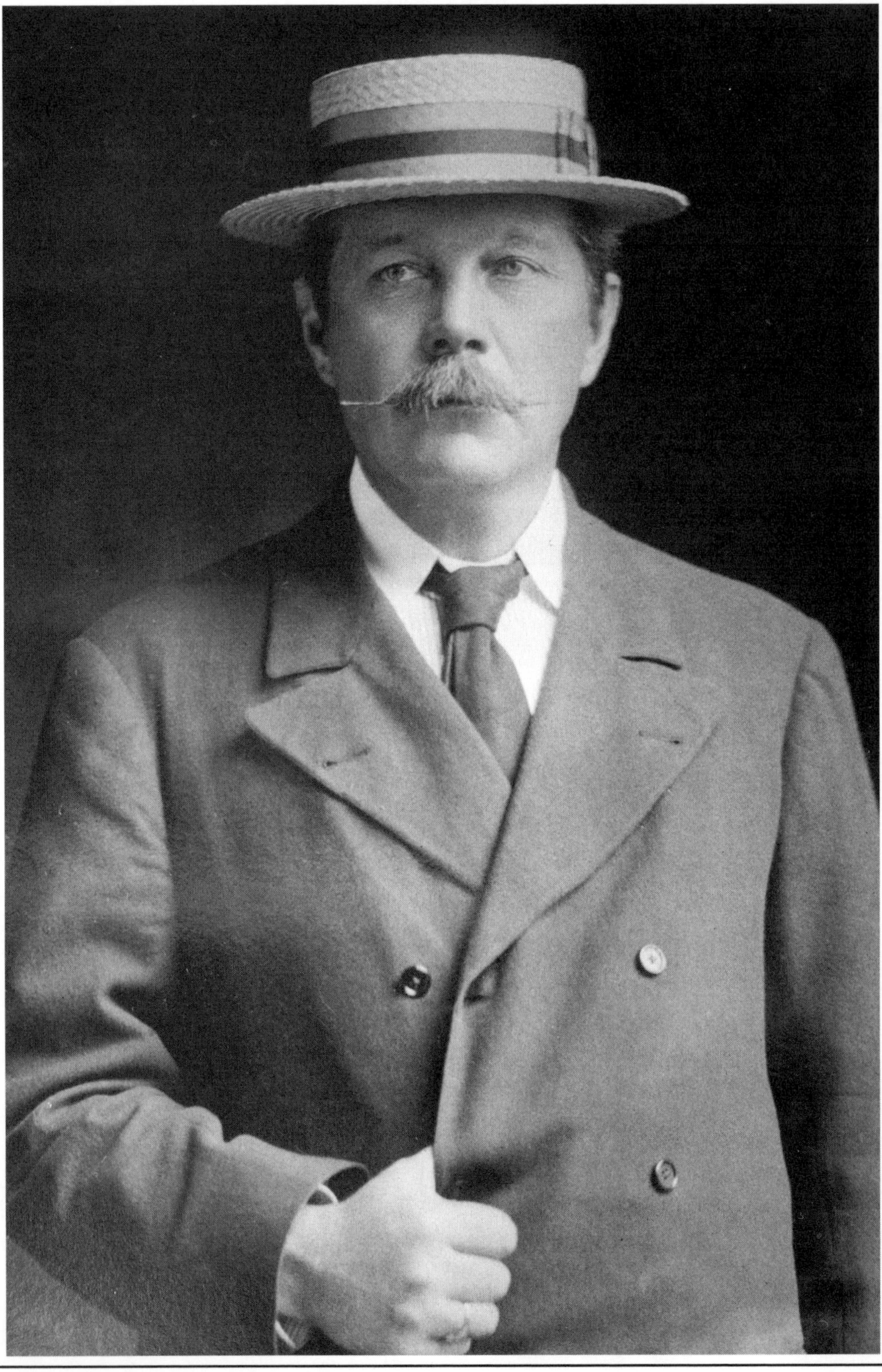

Sir Arthur Conan Doyle

1923

(Second Entry)

What? Could the following have come from the same man who wrote about the evil Brigham Young and his Danites in A Study in Scarlet *(see entry for 1887)? Sherlock Holmes's creator apparently changed his view of the Mormons after visiting them in 1923.*

The [railroad] line ascends again as you approach the Mormon country, until you come to "Soldiers' Summit," which marks the spot where United States troops were placed in order to overawe the Mormons in 1858. They had fairly settled then into their land of promise, and the more violent spirits among them showed a strong disposition to defy the central Government. However, a peace was patched up, and there was no actual fighting. With all respect to the American soldiers, it was, I think, just as well for them, for our own experience has been that the mounted farmer in his own country is an opponent from whom little honour is to be gained. I know America would in the end have crushed the Mormons, but it would have been after a difficult and chequered campaign, and the compromise was a wise one.

Now we ran down into the wonderful Utah Valley, which was hailed by Brigham Young, the moment he saw it from under the canvas tilt of his wagon, as being the promised land. "Stop here! We go no farther," he cried. There is a great deal in the whole story which reminds one of the exodus of the Boers from Cape Colony, and when I saw a group portrait of the surviving pioneers taken in 1897 I seemed to recognize the familiar South African faces, the shaggy-bearded, patriarchal men and the stern, hardworked housewives who cared for them. The flight of the Boers from the British settlements, across the Karroo amid the Kaffirs, is very parallel to the flight of the Mormons from American civilization across the Plains amid the Red Indians, and to match either of them one has to go back to the flight of the Children of Israel from the Egyptians across the desert of Sinai amid the Midianites and the other savage people who opposed them. The old wheel of history is for ever turning. (Doyle, *Our Second American Adventure*, 84–85)

We were amazed as we drove from the station to see what a splendid city the Mormons have raised. As a fact they are only 40 per cent. of the city inhabitants, but they are so united and their average character is so high that they are still predominant, though the Gentile majority rather resent that predominance and are even now organizing to dispute it. In the country round, however, the farmers are 80 per cent. Mormons, so that it is right and proper that the State offices should be nearly all held by members of that faith. I could not find anywhere the least trace of persecution, and a fine spirit of tolerance was shown in many things. The most personal instance was that the Mormon Church had allowed me to speak in their Tabernacle. When I remembered how often I and other Spiritualists have been refused permission to speak in ordinary secular halls which happened to be under the control of some Christian religious body, I could not but contrast the good feeling of the

Sir Arthur Conan Doyle and family on their visit to America

Mormons, who put their own special assembly-hall at my disposal. It was more magnanimous because in my early days I had written in *A Study in Scarlet* a rather sensational and overcoloured picture of the Danite episodes which formed a passing stain in the early history of Utah. This could have been easily brought up to prejudice opinion against me, but as a matter of fact no allusion was made to it save by one Gentile doctor, who wrote and urged me to make some public apology. (86–87)

The interest in my lecture seemed to be very great and 5,000 people at the very lowest estimate assembled in the Tabernacle to hear me. I have never addressed a more responsive and intelligent audience. Both of the papers the next day, in describing the scene, used the expression "spellbound," from which I hope that it was granted to me to rise to the occasion. I had felt very weary since I began to talk in high altitudes, and I was still at 4,000 feet, so for the first time I asked my audience to excuse me in the middle and took five minutes' rest, while the great Mormon organ, one of the greatest in the world, played a beautiful and spiritual voluntary. This new arrangement, introduced between the philosophical and the photographic halves of my lecture, acted very well, and I got through less weary than usual; while as to my audience, one of the papers said the next day that the whole subject had fascinated them so that they lingered behind and would hardly leave the building. When one considers that the whole population of the town is 120,000 and that more than 5,000 were at the lecture, it was certainly a remarkable occasion and a record for any paid performance in the hall.

I would say a word as to the place itself, which is as strange and effective as many other points connected with these wonderful people. It is as big, roughly, as the Albert Hall, but it is shaped like an enormous oval ship upside-down, with a smooth keel for the roof. Perhaps a whale back would be a better simile. No nails were used and it is entirely bolted together with wood. So perfect are the acoustic properties that the least whisper goes to the back of the building, and it is a perfect joy to stand on the rostrum and feel how easily one can command one's audience. (88)

Everything about Salt Lake City seemed to me wonderful and unusual, even the railway-station. Fancy an English railway-station of a city which is not larger than Coventry with two magnificent frescoes spanning each end of the waiting-room. One is of the pioneer band coming through the end of the pass with their wagons, while the leaders look down on the Land of Promise. The other is the joining-up of the trans-continental line

Everything about Salt Lake City seemed to me wonderful and unusual.

in 1869. Each is a really splendid work of art. That is one of the things which our railways must learn from the Americans. They are not there merely as a money-making means of transport. They must adorn cities as well as serve them. If they take the public money, they must give beauty as well as services. When one looks at the great marble station at Washington and then compares it with Waterloo or Victoria, one understands what a gulf separates our ideas and how much we have to learn. (88–89)

I shall always retain a memory of the tolerance and courtesy which I received in Salt Lake City. As to the relations between the Gentiles and Mormons in Utah, I have a document before me signed by all the representative Gentiles, many of them British, which says, "We denounce as absolute lies the charges against the Mormons of sexual immorality, or murder or other depravity, or of tyrannous control in the fields of religion, commerce, morals, or society, and we protest against a continuance of this unfounded and wicked propaganda." This should be noted by a certain section of the British Press. (103–4)

It [the Mormon Church] is, I am told, spreading in Mexico, California, and other places, and I for one think that the world will be none the worse in consequence. (104)

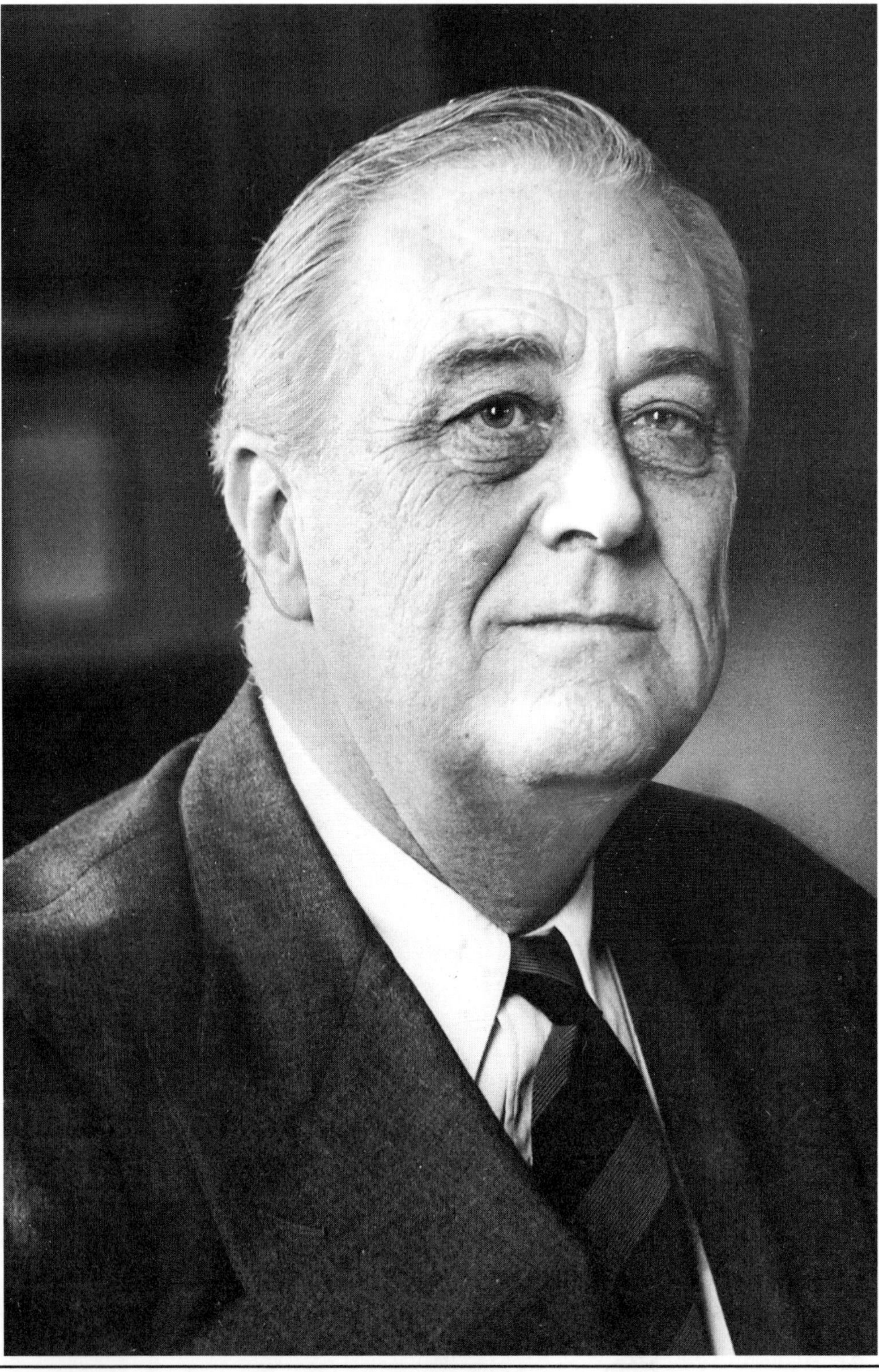

President Franklin D. Roosevelt

1944

President Franklin D. Roosevelt, thirty-second president of the United States, served during the tumultuous years of the Great Depression and World War II. While some Church leaders disagreed with his policies, especially his repealing Prohibition and running for a third term, most Church members supported him and were grateful for his measures to improve the economy. On January 4, 1944, Roosevelt composed this letter to Winston Churchill, prime minister of the United Kingdom, and Churchill's wife, Clementine. Roosevelt enclosed an article on genealogy he'd found in the Deseret News.

> Evidently, from one of the paragraphs, the Dessert News [sic] of Salt Lake City claims there is a direct link between Clemmie and the Mormons. And the last sentence shows that, Winston is a sixth cousin, twice removed, All of this presents to me a most interesting study in heredity.
>
> Hitherto I had not observed any outstanding Mormon characteristics in either of you—but I shall be looking for them from no[w on].
>
> I have a very high opinion of the Mormons—for they are excellent citizens. (*Presidents and Prophets*, 252–53)

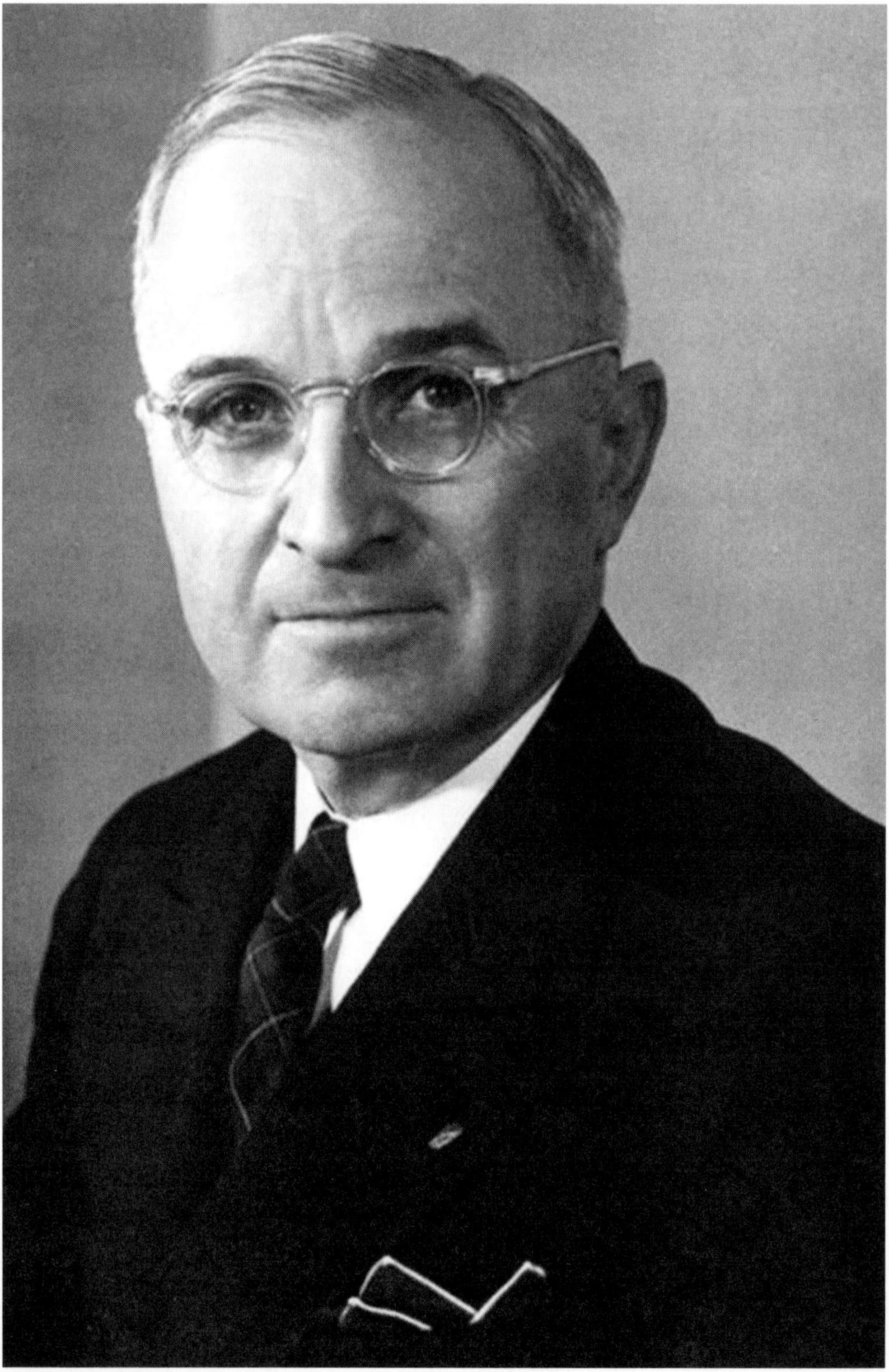

President Harry S Truman

1948

Missouri native Harry S Truman served as a county court judge in Jackson County before becoming a senator and, later, the vice president who took the reins when Franklin D. Roosevelt died in office. His Missouri background meant he had heard of Mormons before, and he appreciated them for the help given his grandfather, as he mentioned in a campaign speech when he stopped in Utah.

I have a close personal interest in the history of this great city. My grandfather, who lived in Jackson County, Mo., was a freighter across the plains, in the early days, and on occasion he brought an ox trainload of goods and merchandise here to Salt Lake City. My grandfather, whose name was Young, went to see Brigham Young, and told him his troubles, and Brigham Young gave him advice and told him to rent space down on the main street here in Salt Lake City, place his goods on display, and he would guarantee that my grandfather would lose no money. And he didn't.

*President Harry S Truman coined the saying "The buck stops here"—
which phrase he put on a small sign that sat on his oval office desk*

Today, I am most cordially received by the President of the Mormon Church, the successor of Brigham Young. I wish my old grandfather could see me now! Those pioneers had faith, and they had energy. They took the resources that Nature offered them, and used them wisely. Their courage and fighting spirit made them secure against enemies. They have left you a great heritage. (*Presidents and Prophets,* 265)

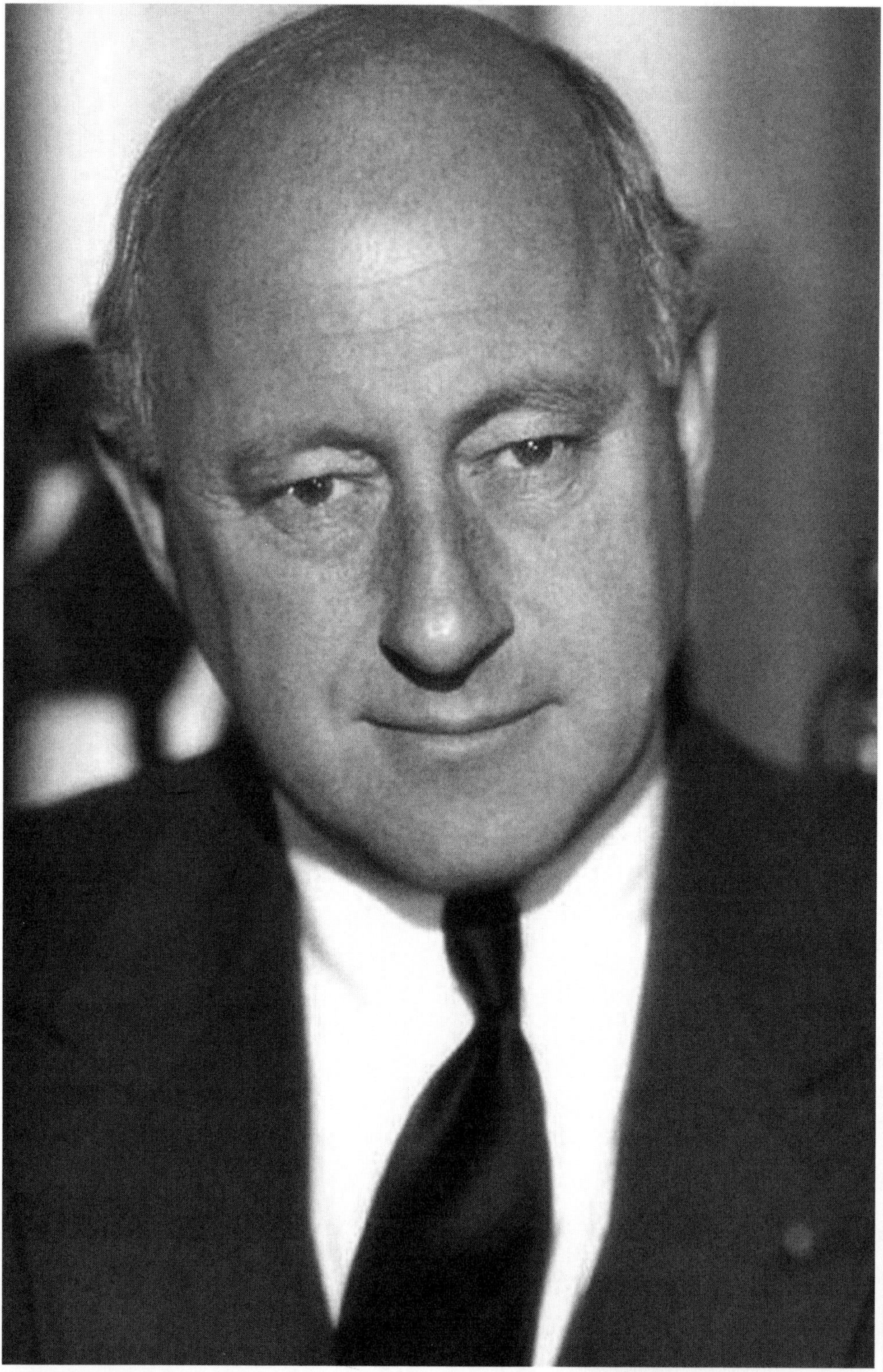

Cecil B. DeMille

1957

On May 31, 1957, movie director Cecil B. DeMille gave the commencement address at Brigham Young University. He had gained fame by directing popular biblical epics like The Ten Commandments, *and he'd gained respect among actors and the public alike for his character. During the McCarthyism era in the 50s, when movie stars were being falsely accused of being communists, DeMille hired blacklisted actors and musicians, thus helping to save their careers. President David O. McKay introduced DeMille by saying, "One element of greatness, we are told, is the ability to choose the right with invincible resolution. Your speaker for this evening has demonstrated in our country that he possesses this virtue. . . . But it is not only in his ability to choose the right that I refer to him as a great man, but because of his soul, his faith in God, his confidence in his fellow men. I love him because of his nobility."*

I have known many members of your Church—and I have never known one who was not a good citizen and a fine, wholesome person—but David O. McKay embodies, more than anyone that I have ever known, the virtues and the drawing-power of your Church.

David McKay, almost thou persuadest me to be a Mormon! And knowing what family life means to the Latter-day Saints, I cannot speak or think of President McKay without thinking too of that gracious and spirited young lady who is his wife.

Only he knows—but the rest of us who know her can guess—what Mrs. McKay has meant to the President and to his work in the years since their lives were joined together "for time and eternity."

The honor you have done me today gives me also a link with another great name in your history—the name that is fittingly borne by this University which he founded, when in 1875 he sent Karl Maeser here to Provo to organize what has now become the keystone of your Church's magnificent educational system.

The name of Brigham Young is great not only in your annals, but in the story of the West and of all America.

Gracious reference has been made this evening to our production of *The Ten Commandments*—which is the story of Moses and the birth of freedom under God. Who can fail to be struck by the similarities between Moses and Brigham Young—between the Exodus of the children of Israel and the Mormon trek across the plains and mountains to this land of Deseret? Moses and Brigham Young were both strong leaders of a strong people.

As the Israelites were brought to Egypt by Joseph, so your people were led to the banks of the Mississippi by another Joseph—but, at Nauvoo and Carthage just as in Goshen, persecution and martyrdom were their lot, until in the providence of God a leader arose to band them together and give them hope and courage and lead them to freedom in a new land. For both, the way was hard—but it was blessed.

When Brigham Young saw the Mississippi River freeze over, letting the ox-carts drive across, how could he fail to think of that earlier time when the Red Sea opened to let the children of Israel walk dry-shod between the walls of water?

Moses and Brigham Young were men of faith, a virile, driving faith—and that faith sustained their people through every hardship.

As Marcus Bach has written of the Mormon pioneers, "Death and burial, birth and pain, tragedy and terror could not hold them back. . . . They fought the weather in every season, battled hostile Indians in every territory and conquered fear of defeat in every company." The children of Israel sang a song of triumph after crossing the Red Sea, when they rested at the oasis that still is called the Well of Moses on the Sinai Peninsula.

The followers of Brigham Young, as they camped in the mud and often had only the bark of trees for food, still could fill the night air of the prairies with song—for nothing could quench the joy born of their vivid faith. They had read in the Book of Mormon, "Men are, that they might have joy"—and to this day that joyousness is one of the most appealing aspects of your faith.

At length they came to that spot now marked by the noble monument dedicated ten years ago—where Brigham Young spoke the historic, prophetic words, "This is the Place." But that was not the end of the Mormon journey, any more than the brink of Jordan was the end of the trail for the Israelites of old. It was not the end for them any more than today is the end of the journey for you, my classmates of 1957. It was their commencement day. . . .

What fills my heart with hope this evening . . . is that I am standing among men and women and talking to young men and women, most of whom

Members of the Famous Players—Lasky Corporation (left to right: Jesse L. Lasky, Adolph Zukor, Samuel Goldwyn, Cecil B. DeMille, and Al Kaufman)

have made their choice, who are committed to the Lord's side, which is also the side of humanity and liberty.

And I am speaking to all of you—not only to the great majority who are Latter-day Saints, but also to the minority who are not. Remember, I am one of that minority here this evening! I am an Episcopalian—but I am speaking to you just as I would to a graduating class of my own Church, or of other Protestants, Catholics, Jews, or Moslems, when I urge you to hold fast to the high conception of Eternal Law which the prophets and teachers of all those faiths have taught.

Like mighty rivers flowing from a single source, all the great religions of the Western world stem from Moses. On their broad streams they carry the precious cargo of their different traditions—but they all share in a common reverence for the Law of God revealed through Moses.

Jesus of Nazareth said "For had ye believed Moses, ye would have believed me." (John 5:46.)

These great religions all teach, as you have been taught here at Brigham Young University, that the Law of God is a law of life—a law of liberty—a law of peace and joy—a law meant not to restrict, but to set free your energies and aspirations for life's highest purposes. All this you know—but there are many in the world who do not know it.

Some of you have gone, others of you will go, out into the world as missionaries of your faith. But whether officially commissioned by the Church or not, all of us have the call to be missionaries, to share with our fellow men the good news that we have heard, the greatness of God and the goodness of His Law.

Our mission field may be a nation—or a neighborhood. That does not matter. To one it may be given to tell that story, ever ancient, ever new, through a medium that will reach hundreds of millions of people for generations. Another's life-work may be accomplished when he plants the seed of truth in the soul of a single child. That does not matter either—for who can say which achievement is the greater? What matters, and matters supremely, is not how many things we do, but what we are.

Emma Ray McKay, Cecil B. DeMille, Charlton Heston as Moses, and LDS Church President David O. McKay on the set of The Ten Commandments *in 1955*

A good tree cannot bring forth evil fruit—and a city set on a hill cannot be hid. If our lives are structured according to the Law of God—if we see His Presence burning in every bush, on every mountainside—if, wherever we are, we can say, "'This is the place' where I am called to serve"—then men will be drawn toward what we stand for, as they were drawn to follow Moses and Brigham Young and other leaders whose lives embodied the eternal principles.

You who belong to the Church of Jesus Christ of Latter-day Saints have a unique tradition to uphold.

Herbert Hoover said, "One of the finest communities in the whole United States sprang from Brigham Young's founding." That is true. Keep it true—by being true. (BYU Commencement Address, 31 May 1957, 2–6)

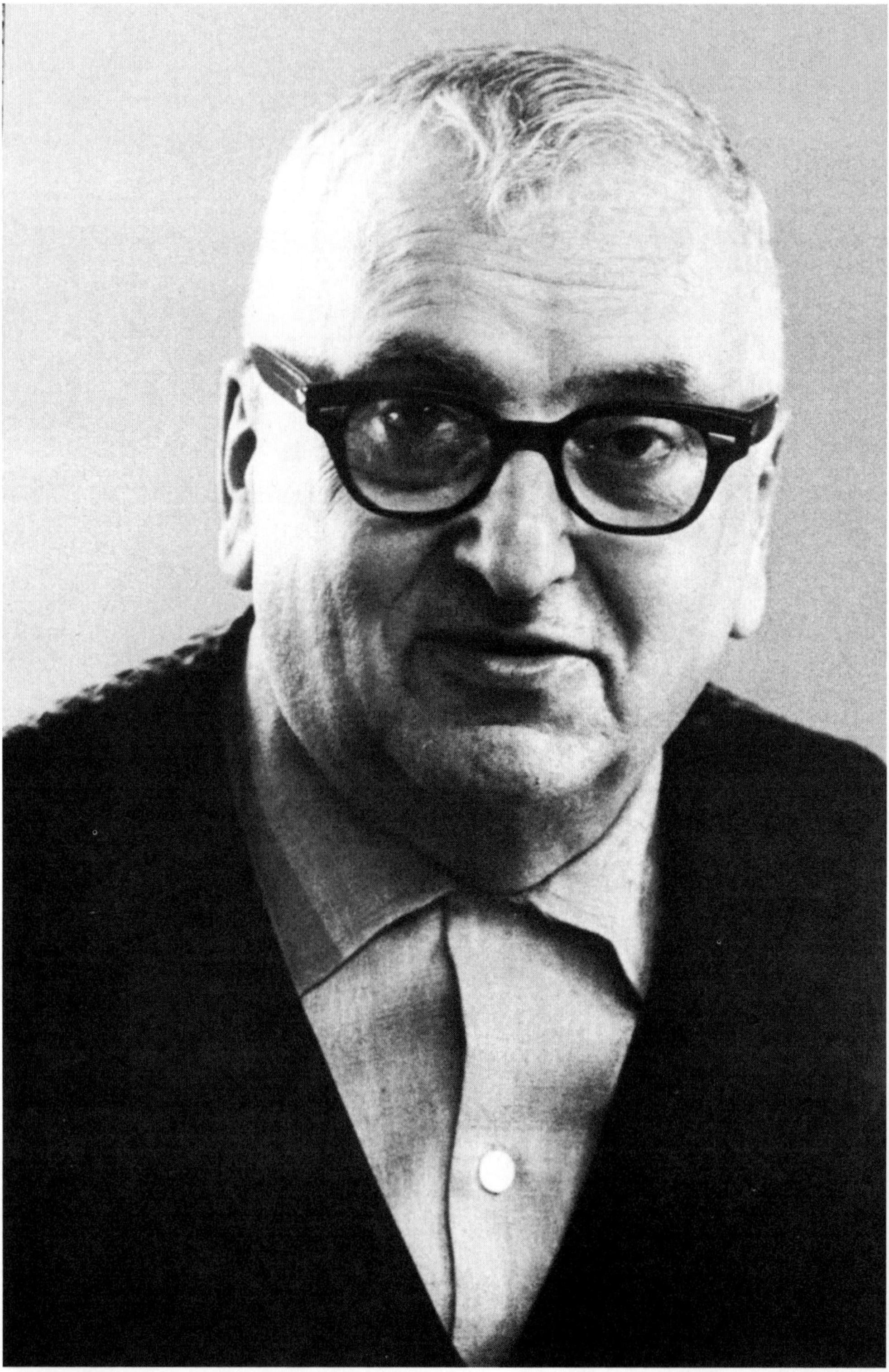

Harry Golden

1959

Harry Golden was a Jewish writer and reporter remembered for his newspaper, the Carolina Israelite, *and his biography of poet Carl Sandburg. He spoke out about racism and traveled abroad to report on world events and to give speeches.*

It is a tremendous honor to be here. It is the largest audience that I have spoken to, and it is a feeling of fulfillment and gratification. The reporter asked me the inevitable question, "How do you like Salt Lake City?" I had never been here before, and it reminds me of a story. Bernard Baruch came to Charlotte one day—his plane was grounded there, it was going someplace else. They checked him into the hotel, and reporters came, and they talked for an hour. "Well," he said, "this city is wonderful, it is great!" Then he said, "What city am I in?"

But I told the reporter something I learned many years ago from the philosopher who said, "A man does not have to leave his room to know the world." I know about Salt Lake City. Oh yes, without ever having been here, I know about it.

I know about it because I know about America. And recently, your good friend, Carl Sandburg, (Ah, what he thinks of you people here, it is a wonderful thing. I am writing his biography, more or less official, and we spend lots of time together. We have a system of equal time, he talks a half hour and I talk a half hour.) when he came back from here, he gave me a beautiful book which you had given him, The Book of Mormon. He said, "This will do you some good, Harry. Read it."

But I have often felt that you people have not had as good a public relations as you deserve, there is no question about that. Brigham Young, for example, has had a bad press all these years. A truly great American deserves much better in our history. Just think of his imagination and his greatness, because it took both to have come in here and to have said, "This is the right place." It has always impressed me tremendously. But he and you have had a bad press.

In this year of 1959, a fellow came through Charlotte, going to Chapel Hill and Duke, a scholar, and he introduced himself to some of the folks, "I am a Mormon." And they asked, "How many wives do you have?" This stereotype, of course, is the very thing we fight against. "How many wives do you have?" is the same as "The Jews have all the money," or "The Negroes are an inferior people." (Harry Golden, "Only in America.")

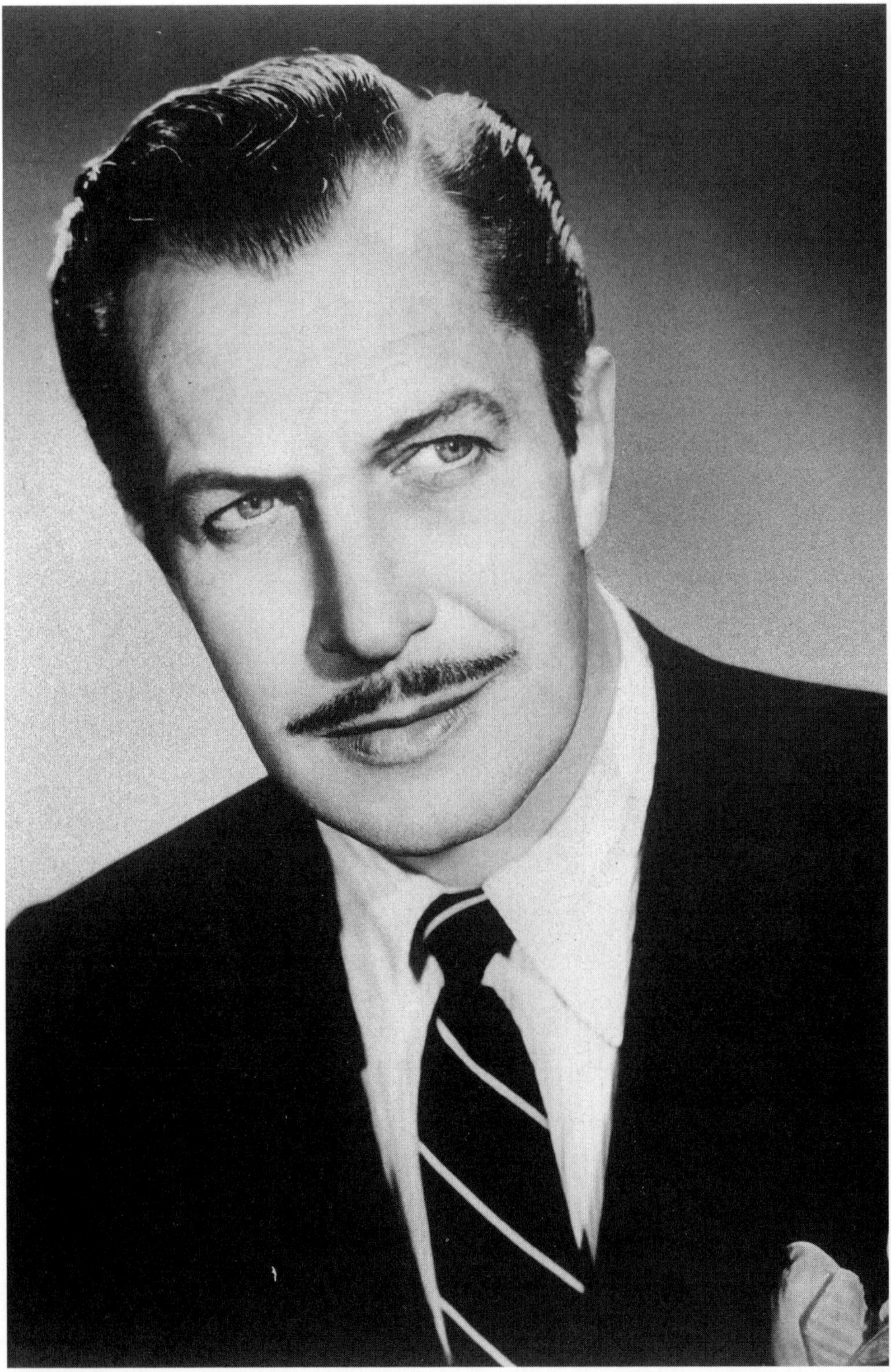

Vincent Price

Vincent Price was a famous Hollywood actor with a distinctive voice, remembered especially for his horror films. Before pursuing film, he majored in fine art and art history, and, as a famous actor, he continued advocating the arts. He donated several fine art pieces to East Los Angeles College, the first community college to own a major art collection. In 1959, Price visited BYU to speak about the arts.

I feel very at home in Utah for I have been here many times. I had the great pleasure a few years ago . . . of playing the part of Joseph Smith in the great motion picture, *Brigham Young*. I had a marvelous correspondence during those years with the late President Heber J. Grant, so believe me, I have the most profound admiration for this state and the wonderful people of this Church. (Vincent Price, "The Enjoyment of Great Art," 2)

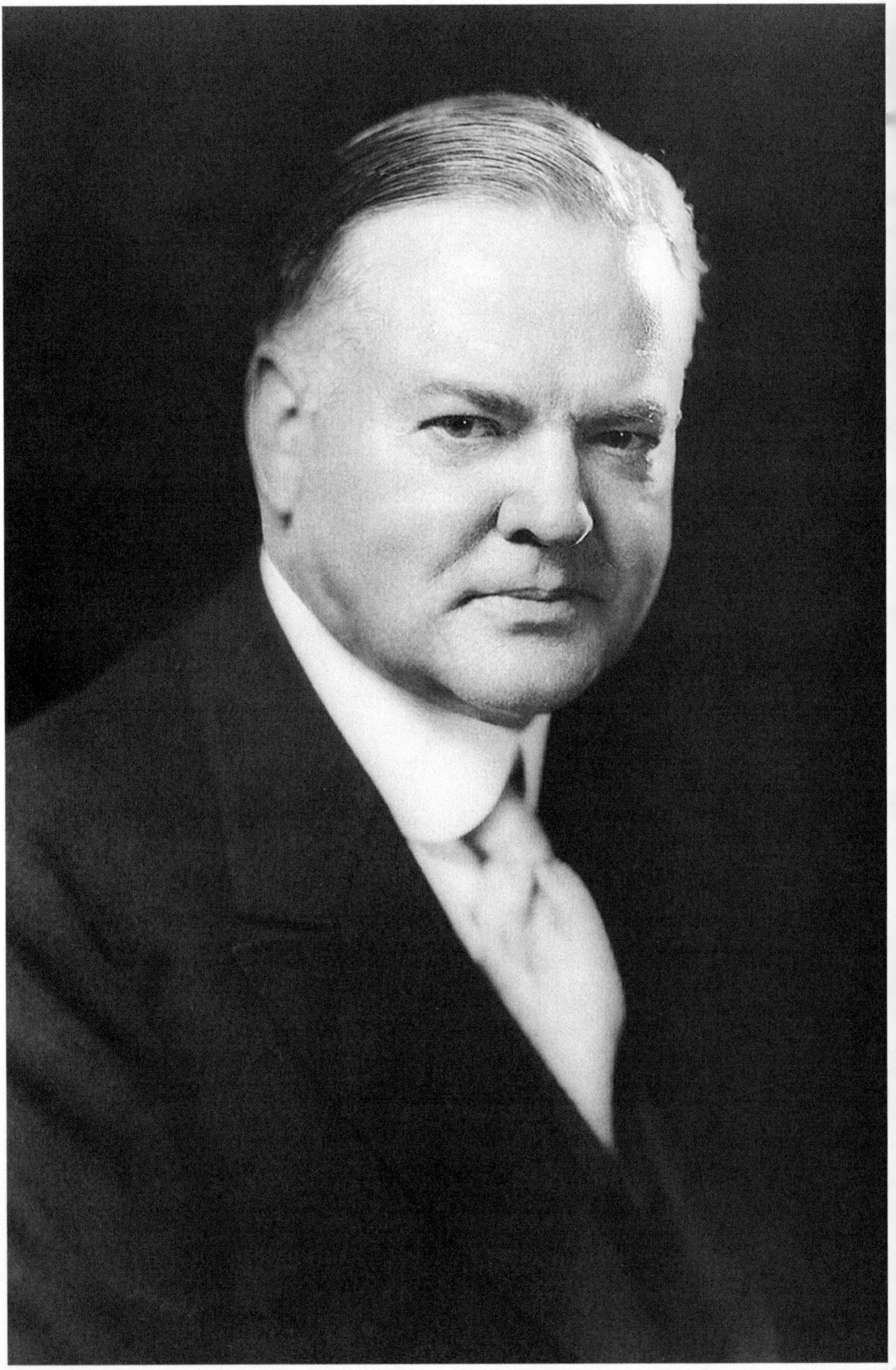

Herbert Hoover

1960

Herbert Hoover served as thirty-first president of the United States, from 1929 to 1933. As the stock market crashed and the Great Depression set in, President Hoover was impressed with the Church's welfare program and commitment to self-reliance. He was such a good friend to LDS Senator and Apostle Reed Smoot that he allowed Elder Smoot to spend his honeymoon at the White House! In 1960, Hoover explained his impressions of the Church. The same year, he agreed to write the foreword to a book of speeches by Ezra Taft Benson.

I have had the great privilege of association with the leaders of the Church of Jesus Christ of Latter-day Saints for more than 43 years. I have witnessed their devotion to public service and their support of charitable efforts over our country and in foreign lands during all these years. I have witnessed the growth of the Church's communities over the world where self-reliance, devotion, resolution and integrity are a light to all mankind. Surely a great message of Christian faith has been given by the Church—and it must continue. (*Presidents and Prophets*, 233–34)

During more than thirty-five years it has been my good fortune to have many associations with the leaders and the members of the faith to which Secretary Ezra Taft Benson was born and to which he adheres.

The religious faiths in our country—all of them—maintain great principles in common. They believe in God. They command the virtue of loyalty to our country. They demand the highest standards of morals, of truth and integrity; the highest performance of public office; a willingness to self-sacrifice for the common good. These principles have in no way been suspended by our gigantic discoveries in science and invention. Secretary Benson is the embodiment of these principles and this faith.

With these principles the religion to which Secretary Benson belongs has pioneered and built a great industrious, law-abiding community. Within it are the highest standards of education and comfort.

From that community have come many of our great religious leaders and statesmen. From them have come a member of the Supreme Court, members of the Cabinet, eminent Senators and Congressmen.

The Church has a special distinction. In times of unemployment and war they have taken care of their own people without charge on the Treasury of the United States. The Church has stood adamant for the Constitution both in business and education. It has also been a staunch supporter of every other basic freedom.

Ezra Taft Benson is today the great contribution of this community to America statesmanship and a leader of the Christian faith. (240, 242)

Former President Herbert C. Hoover in Salt Lake City in the 1950s

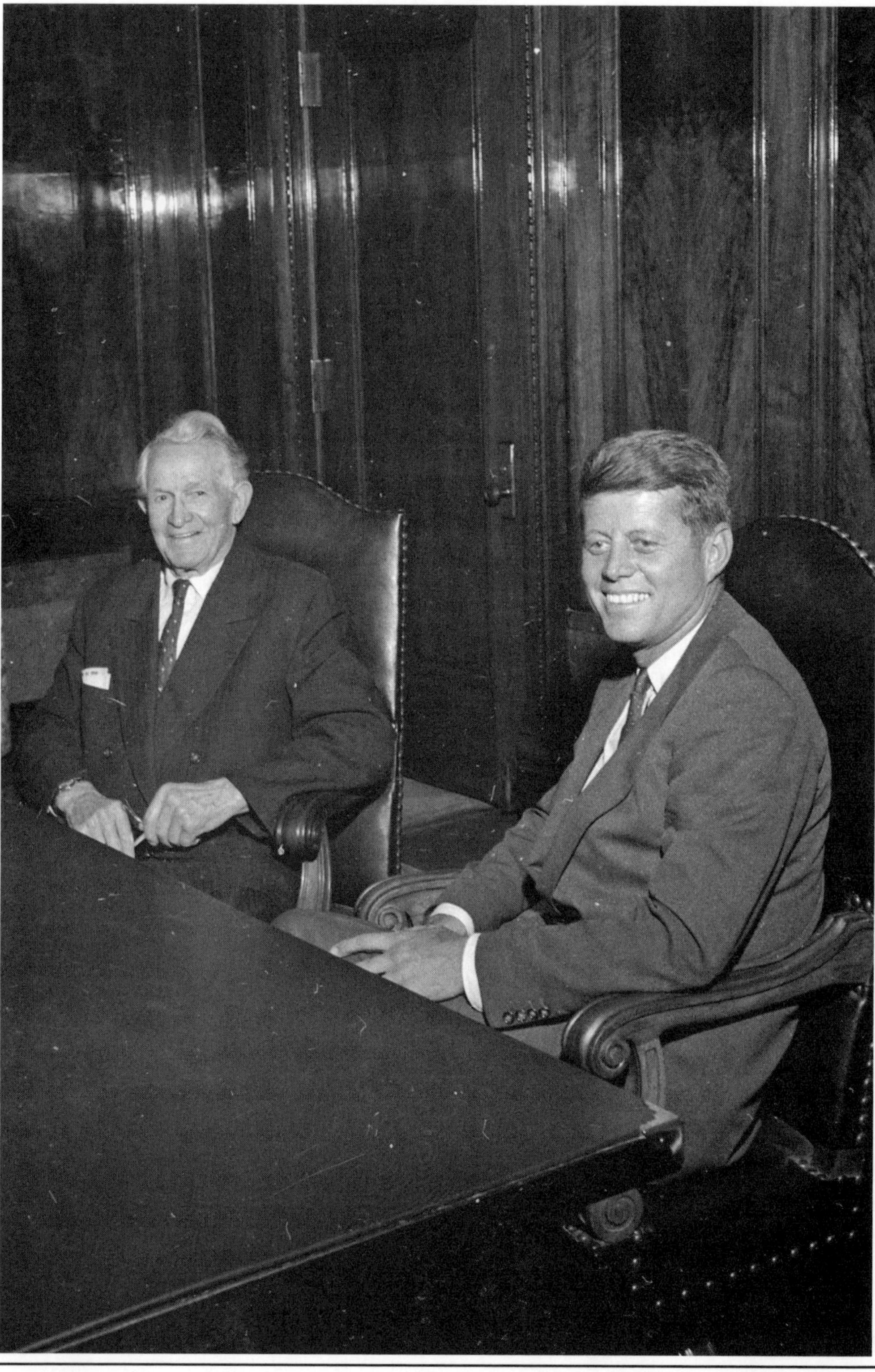

President John F. Kennedy

1960–63

When Senator John F. Kennedy was campaigning for the presidency, he stopped in Utah to deliver a speech about "the New Frontier." As he warned about the dangers of the spread of "godless" communism, he appealed to the faith of Latter-day Saints and called upon them to continue strengthening the nation's moral and spiritual fabric. Kennedy surmounted religious bias during his campaign and became the first Catholic to be elected president of the United States.

I am grateful to the presidency of the Latter Day Saints Church, and to its presiding bishopric, for according me the privilege of speaking within the historic walls of this magnificent tabernacle. This is an honor which I shall long remember.

I am honored, too, to be here with Elbert Curtis, my friend and spokesman in this State. It was here more than a hundred years ago that the great-grandfather of Elbert Curtis declared: "This is the Place." And here Brigham Young built not only a great tabernacle, famed the world over, but a great State, the heart of a great intermountain region, replacing the barren desert with a land now rich in resources, beauty, and spirit.

Tonight I speak for all Americans in expressing our gratitude to the Mormon people—for their pioneer spirit, their devotion to culture and learning, their example of industry and self-reliance. But I am particularly in their debt tonight for their successful battle to make religious liberty a living reality—for having proven to the world that different faiths of different views could flourish harmoniously in our midst—and for having proven to the Nation in this century that a public servant devout in his chosen faith was still capable of undiminished allegiance to our Constitution and national interest.

I am thinking of Apostle Reed Smoot—and those who challenged his right to a seat in the U.S. Senate, charging that he would subordinate the claims of his country to the claims of his church. They did not know—or would not hear—that the 101st section of the Latter Day Saints Doctrine and Covenants gave a scriptural preeminence to the Constitution and its oaths. But fortunately the forces of reason and tolerance enabled him to take his seat. And in the years that followed, Senator Smoot earned the respect and affection of every Senator who had challenged him. He rose to be dean of the Senate and chairman of its powerful Committee on Finance—and no voice was ever heard to say that he had not been devoted solely to the public good as he saw it.

The story of Reed Smoot symbolizes the long struggle of the Mormon people for religious liberty. They suffered persecution and exile, at the hands of Americans whose own ancestors, ironically enough, had fled here to escape the curse of intolerance. But they never faltered in their devotion to the principle of religious liberty—not for themselves alone, but for all mankind. And in the 11th article of faith, Prophet Joseph Smith not only declared in ringing tones: "We claim the privilege of worshipping Almighty God according to the dictates of our own conscience"—he also set forth the belief that all men should be allowed "the same privilege. Let them worship how, where, or what they may."

And what has been true of the Mormons has been true of countless other religious faiths—Jews, Quakers,

Presidential candidate Senator John F. Kennedy speaking in the Tabernacle in September 1960

Catholics, Baptists, Unitarians, Christian Scientists, Seventh Day Adventists, Jehovah's Witnesses, and many, many others. All encountered resistance and oppression. All stuck by both their rights and their country. And in time the fruits of liberty were theirs to share as well; and the very diversity of their beliefs enriched our Nation's spiritual strength. (From a speech by Senator John F. Kennedy in Salt Lake City, Utah, Mormon Tabernacle, on 23 September 1960)

On September 26, 1963, Kennedy delivered another speech in the Tabernacle. Less than two months after hosting President Kennedy for breakfast the morning after his speech, President

President John F. Kennedy with LDS Church President David O. McKay on his left and U.S. Senator Ted Moss on his right, in the Tabernacle in September 1963

David O. McKay mourned Kennedy's assassination in Dallas on November 22, 1963. President McKay stated: "I am deeply grieved and shocked beyond expression at this tragedy. In behalf of the Church in all the world, I express sincere sympathy to Mrs. Kennedy, their children, and all of the close relatives and friends. . . . Only a few weeks ago it was our privilege to entertain the President, and now to think that he has gone we are stunned as well as shocked." (*Presidents and Prophets*, 296)

> Of all the stories of American pioneers and settlers, none is more inspiring than the Mormon trail. The qualities of the founders of this community are the qualities that we week in America, the qualities which we like to feel this country has, courage, patience, faith, self-reliance, perseverance, and, above all, an unflagging determination to see the right prevail. . . .
>
> Let us remember that the Mormons of a century ago were a persecuted and prosecuted minority, harried from place to place, the victims of violence and occasionally murder, while today, in the short space of 100 years, their faith and works are known and respected the world around, and their voices heard in the highest councils of the country. As the Mormons succeeded, so America can succeed, if we will not give up or turn back. (292)

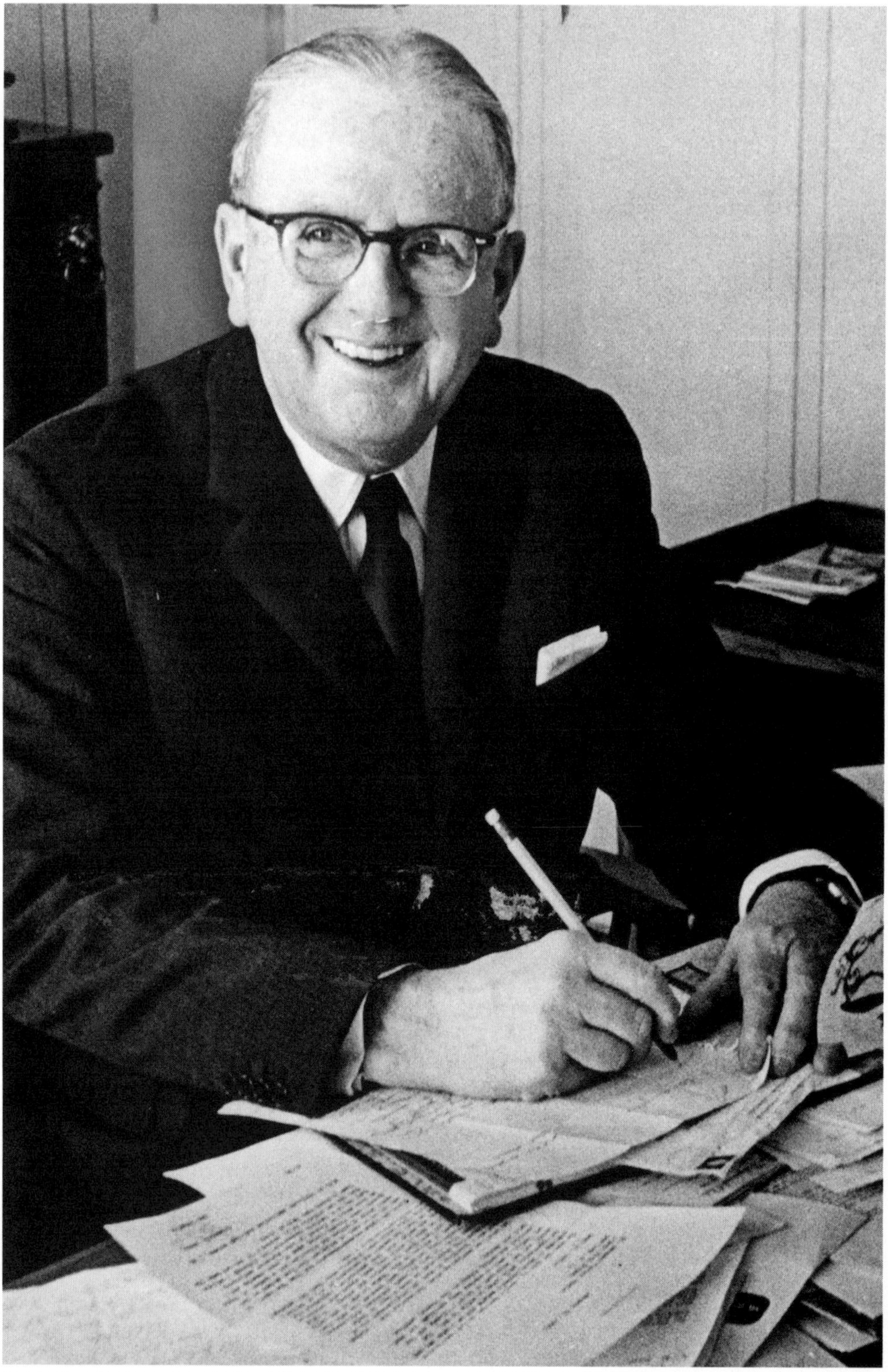

Norman Vincent Peale

1963

Norman Vincent Peale was a Protestant minister who was also a best-selling author. He advocated positive thinking and is sometimes credited for coining the phrase, "When life hands you a lemon, make lemonade." Given his gift for optimism, it's not surprising he was delighted with what he found at Brigham Young University.

I have been on the go ever since I met President Wilkinson and have made a very wonderful survey of this University. I can only say that I think you students ought to be, if you are not, happy and proud that you could come to such a place as this. Indeed, my wife said to me, "Why didn't we send one of our children to Brigham Young University?" because you have here marvelous physical equipment. You have great scholarly leadership. You have the most dramatic and lovely setting for a university that I think I have ever seen in all of my life, with these surrounding and encompassing glorious hills. But, above all, you have here deep, fundamental convictions of the necessity and the place of religion, not only in the life of our time, but also in the educational process. ("Why Positive Thinkers Get Positive Results," 3)

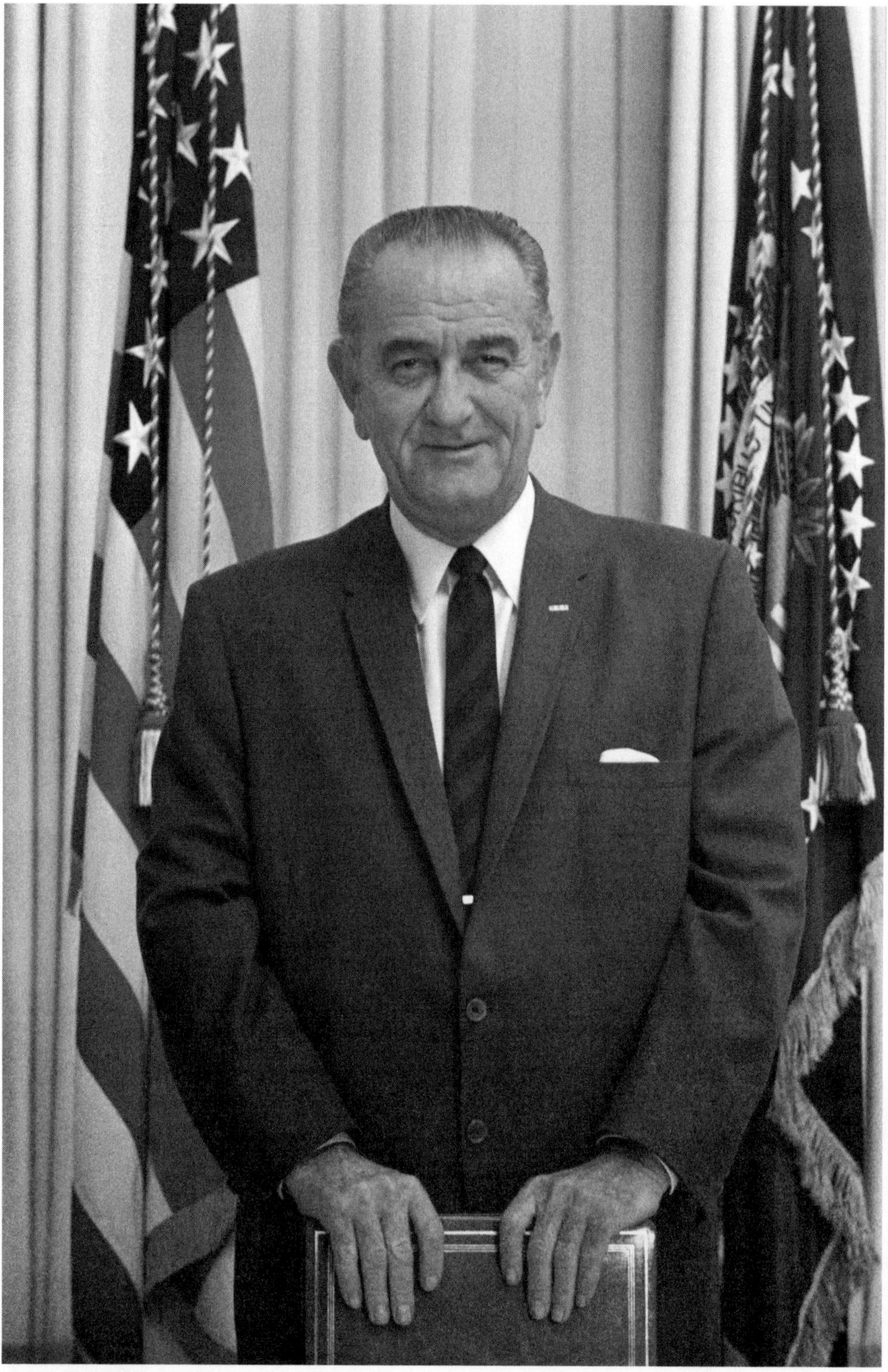

President Lyndon B. Johnson

1964

David O. McKay was the first religious leader President Lyndon B. Johnson invited to visit the White House in 1964, only a few months after President Kennedy had been assassinated. Later that year, President Johnson dropped in on the McKays on his way to California. Soon after he wrote the following note to President Mckay. Apostle Boyd K. Packer quotes President Johnson as once having said, "I don't know just what it is about President McKay. I talk to . . . all of the others [preachers from other faiths] but somehow it seems as though President McKay is something like a father to me. It seems as though every little while I have to write him a letter or something." (Presidents and Prophets, 308)

> Strong friendships seldom depend upon frequency of visits for their strength and meaning. While we have had too few occasions to be with you, both Lady Bird and I draw deep strength and inspiration from our bonds with you. I felt that strength especially last week as we flew back to Washington after meeting with you. (305)

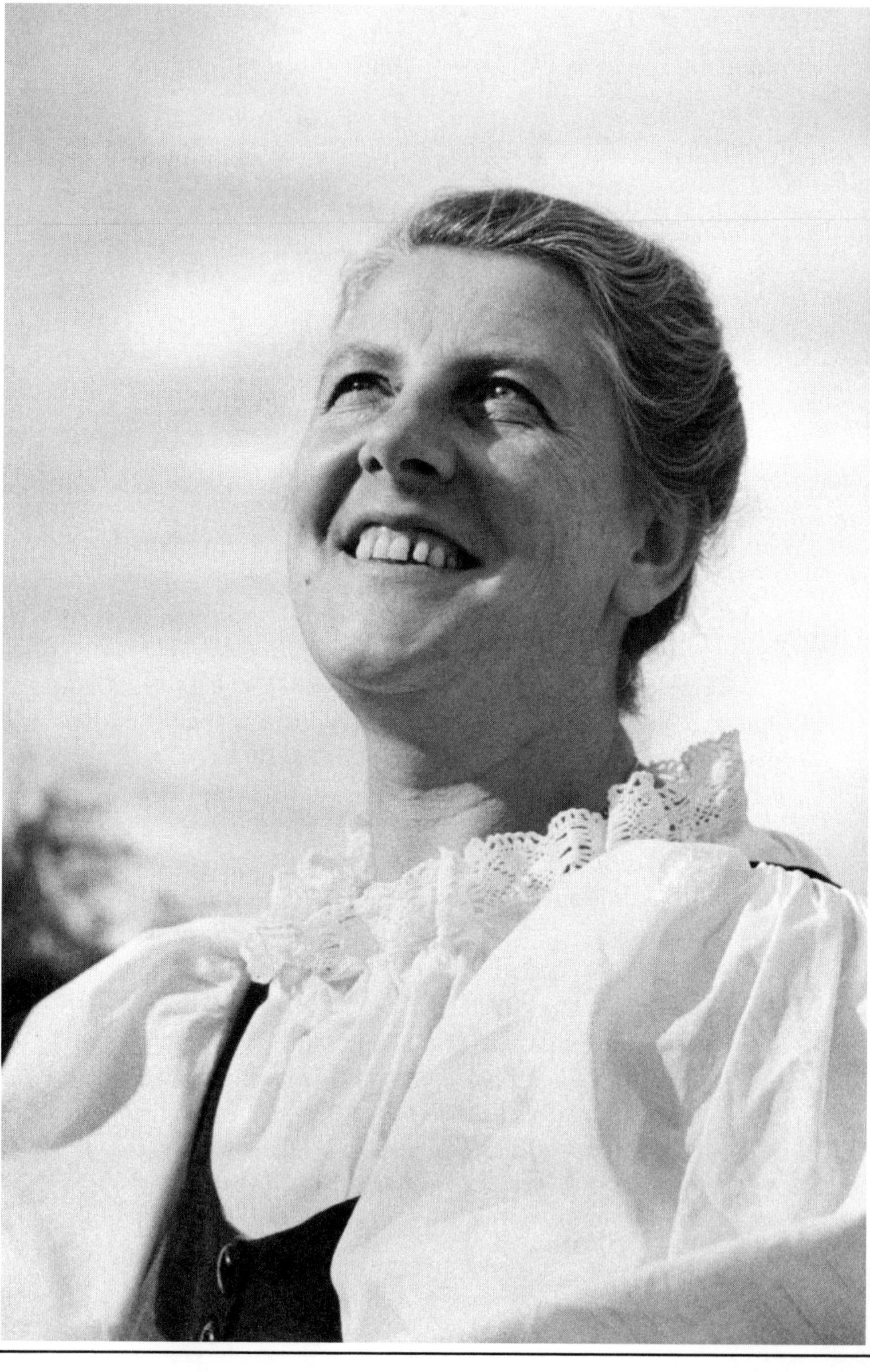

Maria von Trapp

1965

Maria von Trapp gained fame after Rodgers and Hammerstein made a musical, The Sound of Music, *based on her life. She aimed to become a nun but instead married a Navy captain and became the stepmother of seven musically talented children. Following the Trapps' escape from Nazi-occupied Austria, they earned money singing across Europe until they were able to immigrate to the United States. They continued singing and touring as the Trapp Family Singers. Wherever they went, Maria recognized the Mormon missionaries.*

In Brazil, in Argentina, in Peru, in Chile, in Mexico, in New Zealand, in Australia . . . whenever there were two strapping young Americans—two—coming up to us, very friendly, they were Mormon missionaries. I always admired the Mormon Church, for this in a way is a most natural thing to do, to give two years of your life—a preconceived Peace Corps plan, long before there was a Peace Corps—and to go to teach all people, as He has told us to do. (*The Real Story of Maria von Trapp*, 6)

Arctic Ocean
UNION
NORTH
CANADA
AMERICA
UNITED
STATES
MEXICO
EAST INDIES

Paul Harvey

1967

Paul Harvey was a famous news commentator for ABC Radio Networks, and a voice millions recognized not only for sharing the news but also for seamlessly plugging sponsors' products. He won numerous awards, including the Presidential Medal of Freedom in 2005. President James E. Faust explained how, after visiting an LDS school campus, Harvey observed the following:

> Each . . . young face mirrored a sort of . . . sublime assurance. These days many young eyes are prematurely old from countless compromises with conscience. But [these young people] have that enviable headstart which derives from discipline, dedication, and consecration. (James E. Faust, "The Light in Their Eyes," 20)

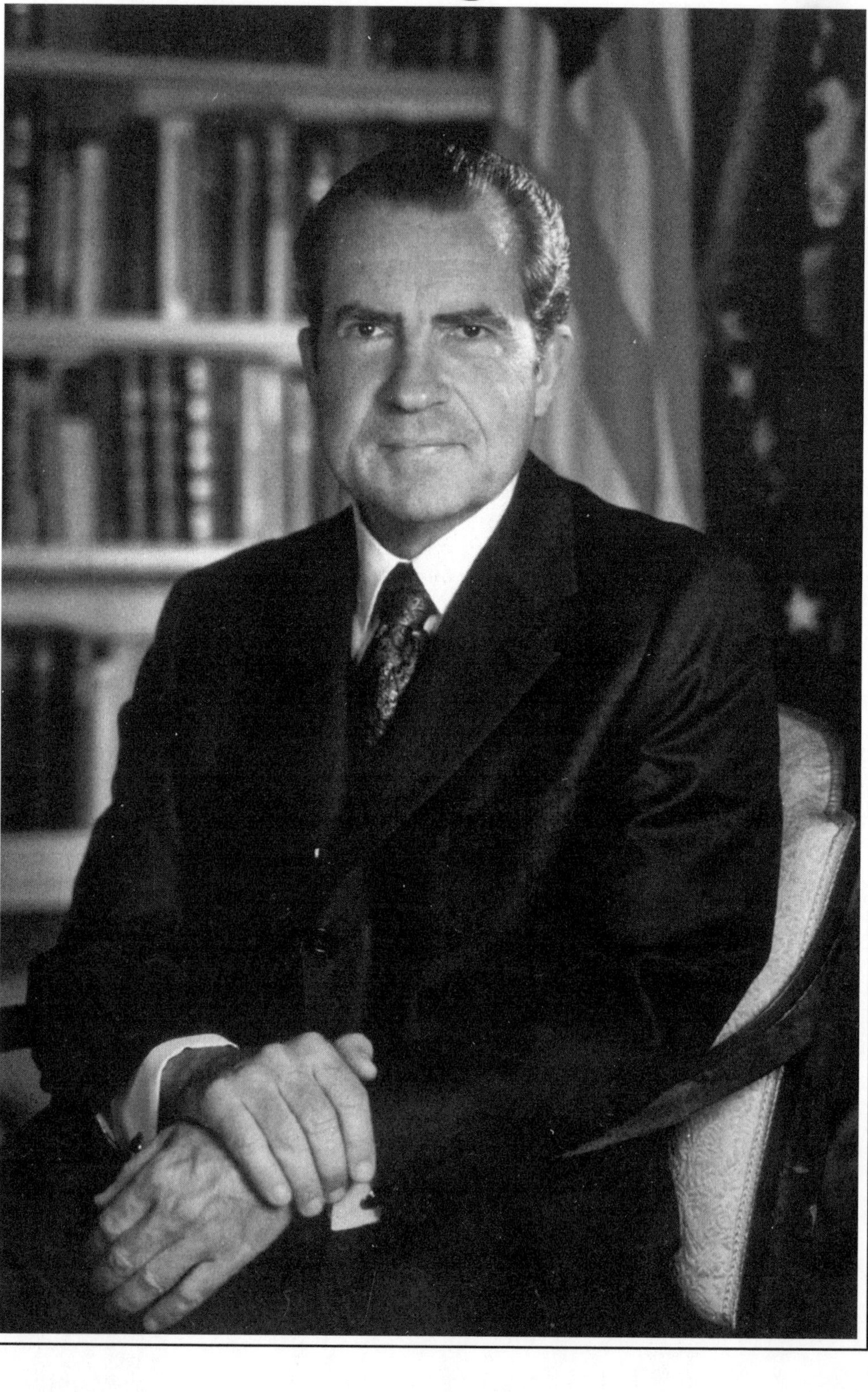

President Richard M. Nixon
1970

Long before Richard M. Nixon was exposed for dishonesty and removed from office, he had the support of Utah Mormons. He enjoyed visiting Utah because he could always count on being welcomed. In 1970, he gave two speeches to the Mormons, one from the steps of the Administration Building on Pioneer Day, and another in the Tabernacle on Halloween.

Pioneer Day means something to the people of Utah but it also means something to the people of America, because the pioneers who came here taught other pioneers who went on through the balance of the West. And it is that kind of spirit, the kind of spirit that sees a great problem but the greater the problem puts in great effort, the kind of spirit that doesn't blame adversity on somebody else but tries to do something about it himself. That is what built this State; that is what built America. . . . Thank you for giving America such a fine lesson. . . .

I do not know of any group in America . . . who have contributed more to that strong, moral leadership and high moral standards—the spirit

Above: President Richard M. Nixon meets with the LDS Church's First Presidency in July 1970. Below: President Nixon speaks at the Tabernacle on July 24, 1970. President Joseph Fielding Smith at the left.

that has kept America going through bad times as well as good times; no group has done more than those who are members of this Church. I want to thank you for what you've done for the spirit of America. . . . If you can continue those spiritual values, I'm sure America is going to go ahead and do very well. (*Presidents and Prophets,* 320–21)

A distant view of Richard Nixon in the Tabernacle on Pioneer Day in 1970

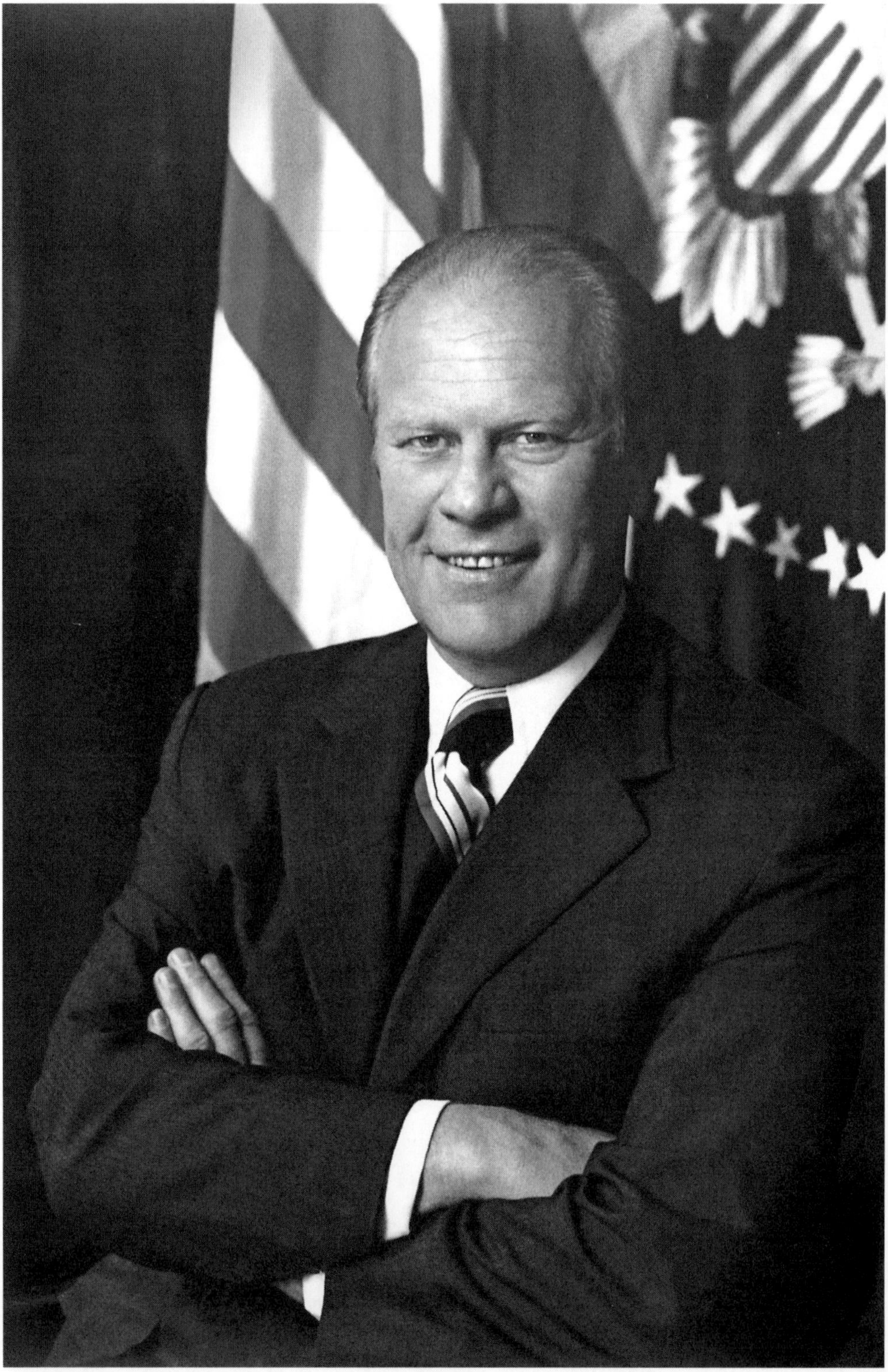

President Gerald R. Ford

1974–78

When Gerald Ford was vice president of the United States, he visited Utah State University to give the commencement address. He also visited Temple Square, met with the First Presidency, and commended President Kimball for the goodness of Utah's people. Later, following his presidency, he commented on being given a biography of Spencer W. Kimball.

You should be proud of the great work ethic that is such a vital part of the lifestyle of the people of Utah. You should be proud of the high moral principles which in many respects are an example to all of us who live in the other 49 states. Let me say we've appreciated very much the warmth of the welcome we've had here on this visit. It's been a great experience for Mrs. Ford and myself, and we look forward to returning because we like people from Utah; we like your country, and we like what you stand for. (*Presidents and Prophets,* 328)

3 July 1979: On the eve of the nation's bicentennial, President Ford (left) and Spencer W. Kimball (right) were greeted by one hundred Primary children, on the White House lawn, who sang "I Am a Child of God."

President Spencer W. Kimball in his office at the Church Administrative Building with President Gerald R. Ford in 1977

I have visited with Spencer W. Kimball on several occasions and I consider him to be one of the great spiritual leaders of the world. His life has been a sermon that mankind could emulate. I am grateful to have this biography to learn even more about this great spiritual leader. I have visited Salt Lake City on many occasions and I have several Mormon friends. I really respect the principles, the traditions and the dedication of the Mormon people. (332)

> *I consider him to be one of the great spiritual leaders of the world.*

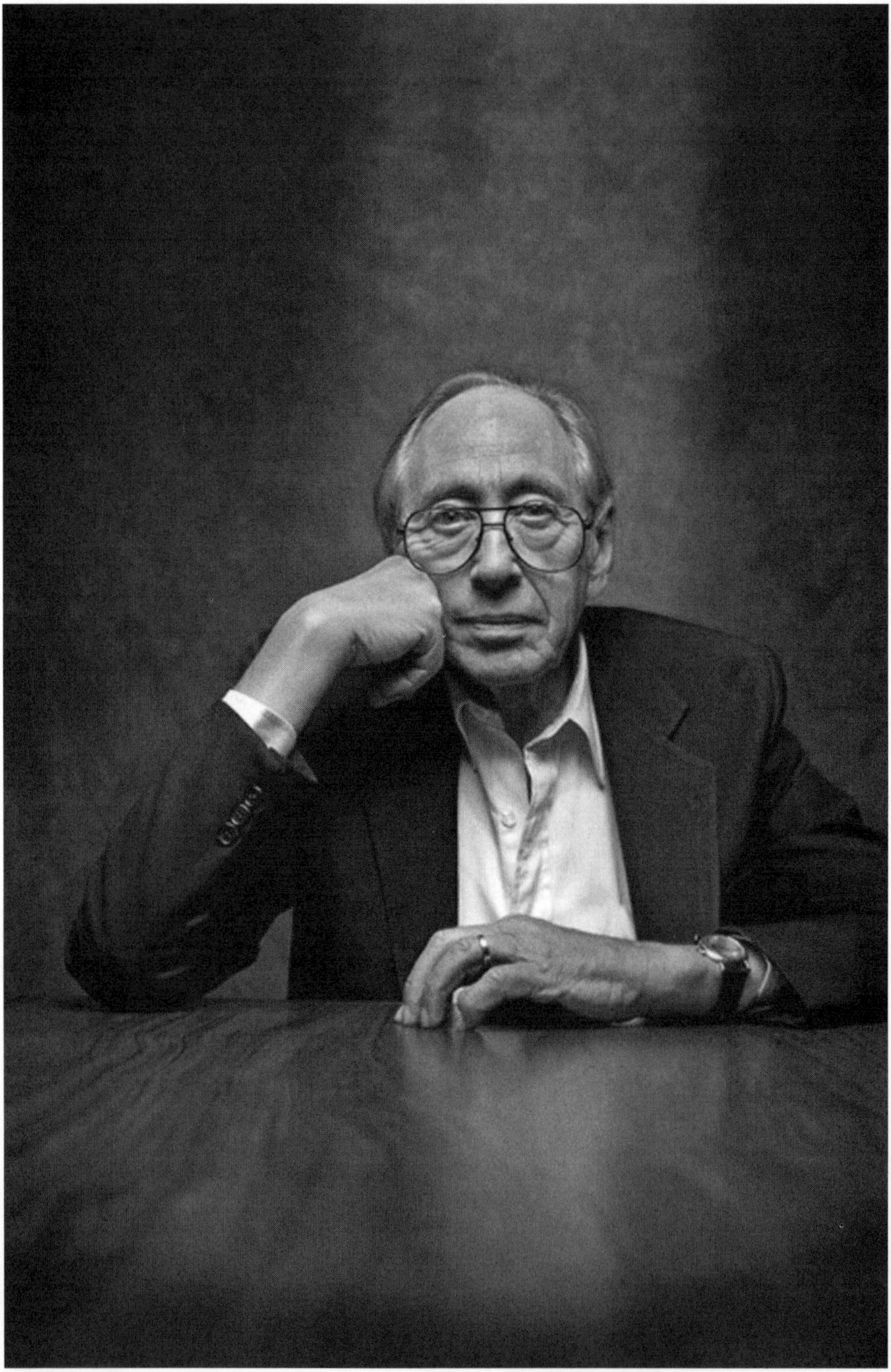

Alvin Toffler

1980

American writer and former associate editor of Fortune Magazine, *Alvin Toffler wrote about the future. In his book,* The Third Wave, *about post-industrial society, he held up the Mormons' tendency toward self-sufficiency as "another clue to possible future lifestyles."*

Many Mormon stakes—a stake corresponds to, say, a Catholic diocese—own and operate their own farms. Members of the stake, including urban members, spend some of their free time as volunteer farmers growing food. Most of the produce is not sold but stored for emergency use or distributed to Mormons in need. There are central canning plants, bottling facilities, and grain elevators. Some Mormons grow their own food and take it to the cannery. Others actually buy fresh vegetables at the supermarket, then take them to the local cannery.

Says a Salt Lake City Mormon, "My mother will buy tomatoes and can them. Her relief 'society,' the women's auxiliary society, will have a day and they'll all go and can tomatoes for their own use." Similarly, many Mormons not only contribute money to their church but actually perform volunteer labor—construction work, for example.

None of this is to suggest that we are all going to become members of the Mormon church, or that it will be possible in the future to re-create on a wide scale the social and community bonds one finds in this highly participatory yet theologically autocratic group. But the principle of production for self-use, either by individuals or by organized groups, is likely to spread farther. (Alvin Toffler, *The Third Wave*, 298)

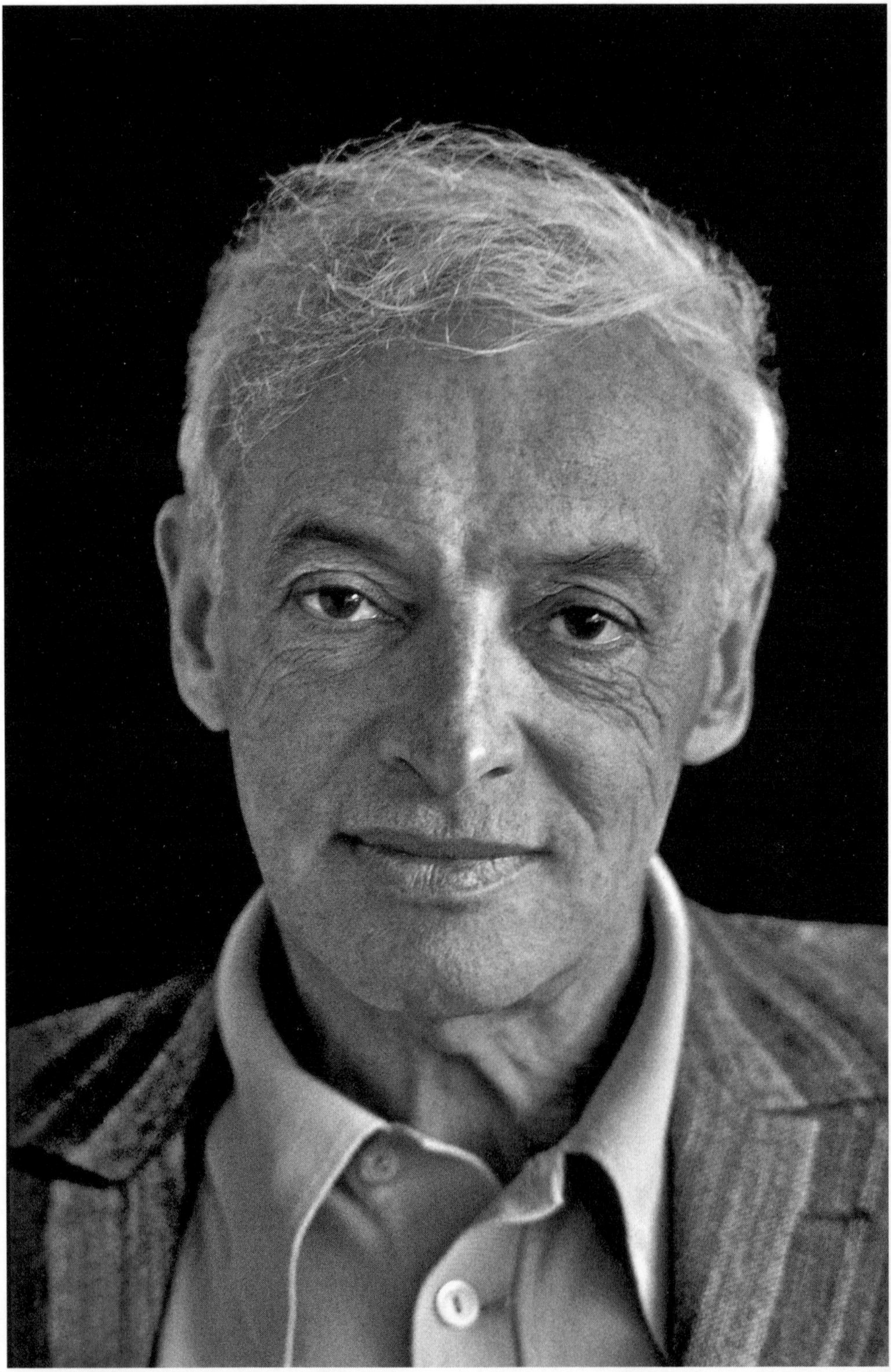

Saul Bellow
1994

Canadian-American journalist, novelist, and playwright Saul Bellow was born to Jewish-Russian parents near Montreal and was raised in Chicago. He won just about every prestigious literature award that exists: the National Book Award (three times!), the Pulitzer, and the Nobel. While his writing often reflects deep themes such as the meaning of life, he didn't seem to connect with the Mormon faith as much as he was intrigued by the people. In one of his essays he shared his experience in meeting a Mormon missionary in Nauvoo.

On the Mississippi a few hours south of Galena, the Mormons built a city at Nauvoo in 1839 and erected a temple. After the murder of the prophet Smith and his brother in neighboring Carthage, the Mormons emigrated under the leadership of Brigham Young, leaving many empty buildings. Into these came a band of French communists, the Icarians, led by Étienne Cabet. Their colony soon failed; discord and thefts broke it up. Cabet died in Saint Louis, obscurely. And after the Icarians came German immigrants, who apparently sobered up the town.

Now, unobtrusively but with steady purpose, the Mormons have been coming back to Nauvoo. They have reopened some of the old brick and stone houses in the lower town, near the Mississippi; they have trimmed the lawns and cleaned the windows, and set out historical markers and opened views on the river, which here, as it approaches Keokuk Dam, broadens and thickens with mud. Sunday speedboats buzz unseen below the bend where the brown tide, slowly hovering, turns out of sight.

Nauvoo today is filled, it seemed to me, with Mormon missionaries who double as tourist guides. When I came for information I was embraced, literally, by an elderly man; he was extremely brotherly, hearty and familiar. His gray eyes were sharp, though his skin was brown and wrinkled. His gestures were wide, ample, virile, and Western, and he clapped me on the back, as we sat talking, and gripped me by the leg. As any man in his right mind naturally wants to be saved, I listened attentively, but less to his doctrines perhaps than to his Western tones, wondering how different he could really be from other Americans of the same type. I went to lie afterward beside the river and look at Iowa on the other bank, which shone like smoke over the pungent muddy water that poured into the southern horizon. (Saul Bellow, *It All Adds Up*, 200)

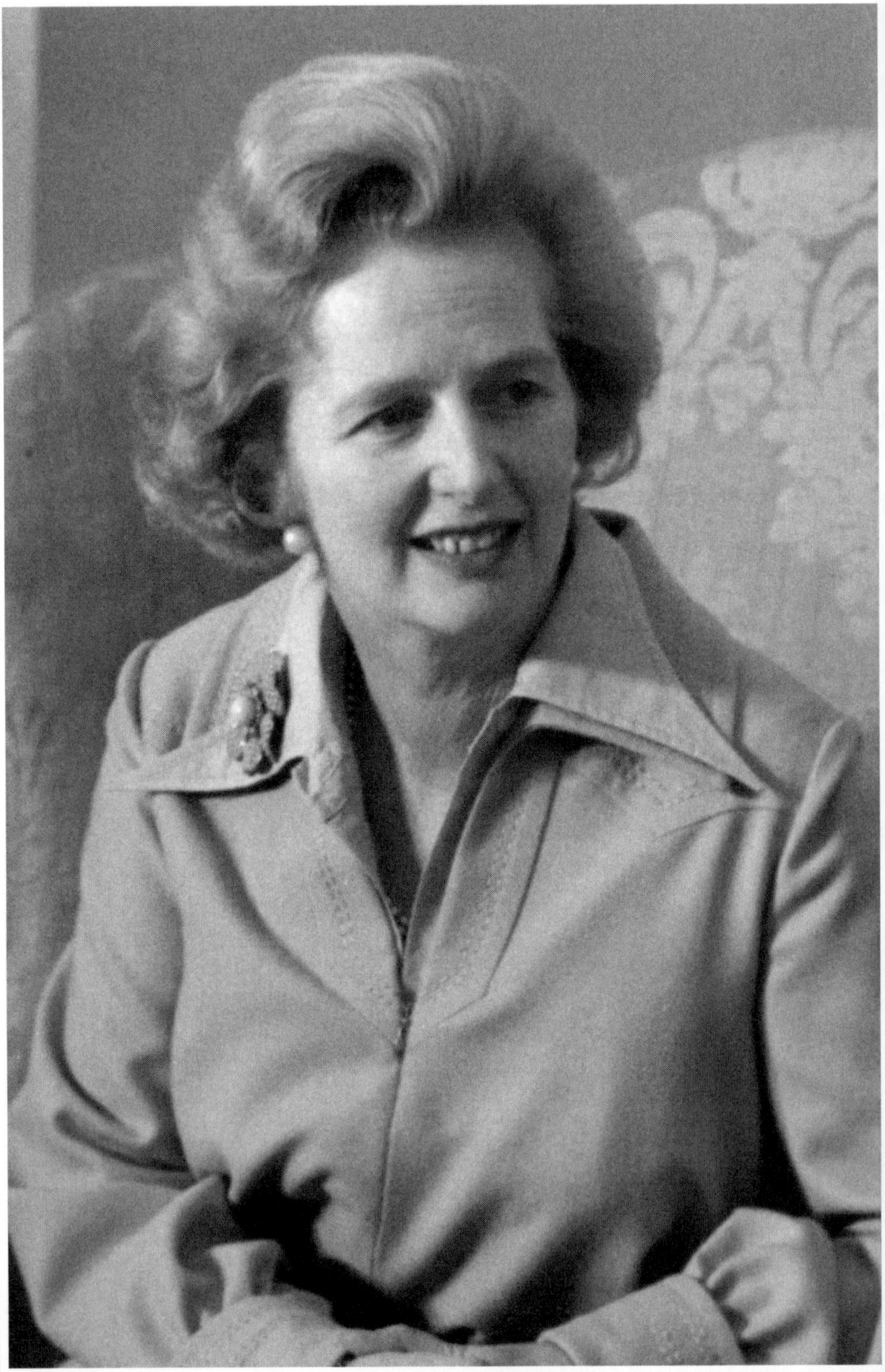

Margaret Thatcher

1996

Margaret Thatcher served longer than any other prime minister in Great Britain and was the country's first woman to be elected to that position. During her three terms, she supported measures to increase free-market economy, decrease the influence of labor unions, control inflation, and decrease government welfare. She was a staunch ally of President Ronald Reagan in opposing the spread of communism. Following her retirement from politics, she spoke at Brigham Young University.

So often the hour produces the leader. And, led by Brigham Young, the Mormon pioneers made the long journey to found this state. They were self-reliant, hardworking, honorable, and determined to overcome all difficulties. They suffered much, but their faith brought them through all the adversity. It was that kind of faith, that courage, that infused the life of this new nation destined to become uniquely great. Yours is a most remarkable story of faith in action, and it changed the world. ("The Moral Challenges for the Next Century," 5 March 1996)

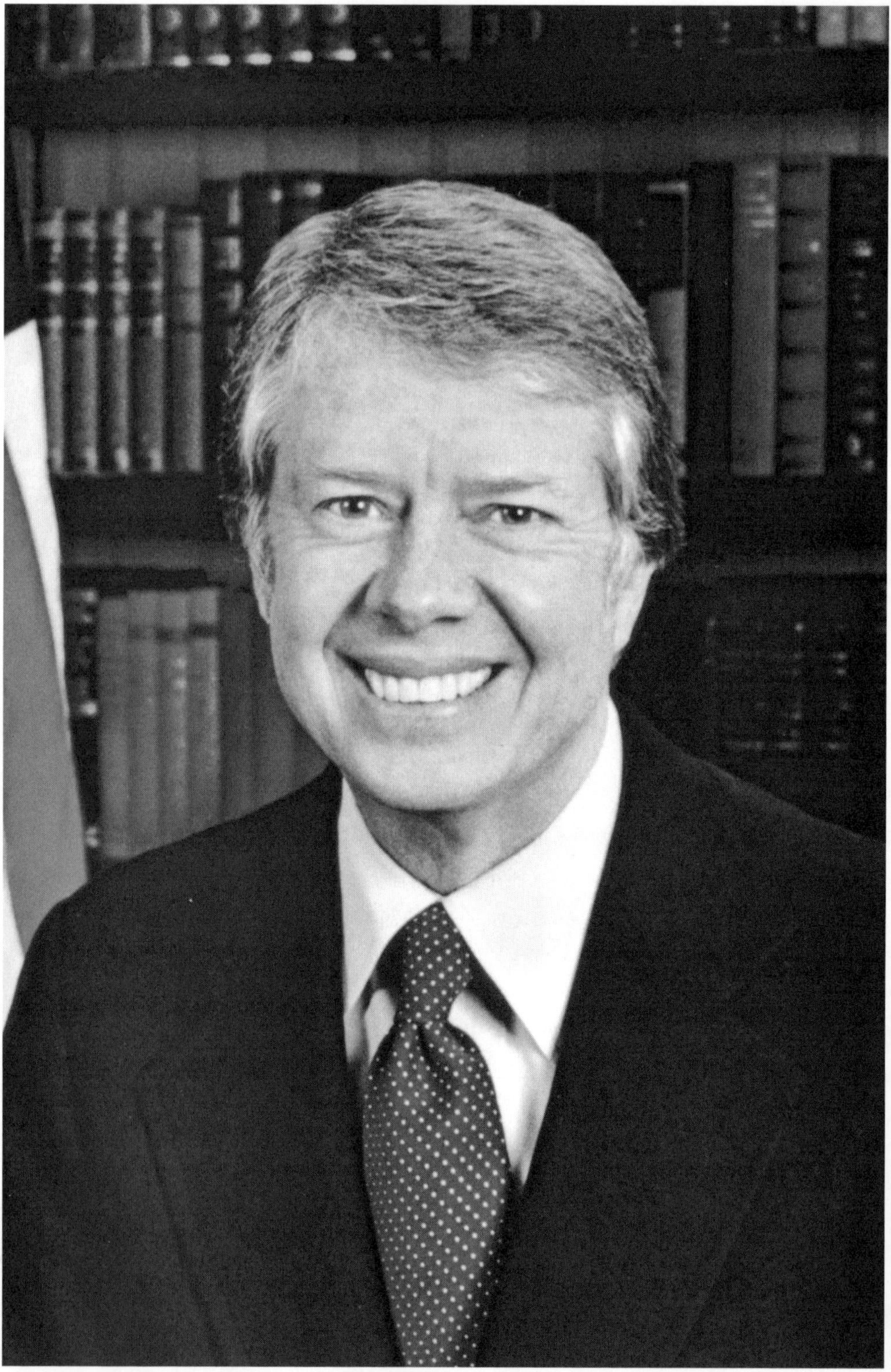

Jimmy Carter

2004

After serving as the thirty-ninth president of the United States, Jimmy Carter kept himself busy promoting international peace; winning the Nobel Peace Prize; writing poetry, essays, and novels; and—with a little help from the First Presidency of the LDS Church—delving into his family history.

We've relished the private excursions with just our immediate family, but there are times, especially in the South, when larger gatherings are the custom. Although three branches of Rosalyn's family, the Smiths, Murrays, and Wises, have enjoyed regular reunions for several generations, my parents' relatives never had either the interest or perhaps the courage to congregate all the Gordys or Carters in the same place at the same time. While I was in the White House, Mormon leaders brought me a genealogical record of my ancestors in America back to the early 1600s. It was in orderly file folders and summarized in a leather-bound book, but I never paid it much attention until after we returned to Plains. Someone sent me "Family Tree Maker" computer software, and I entered the data in the program.

Later, one of my cousins and I decided to have a reunion of the direct descendants of our great-great-grandfather Wiley Carter, who was born in 1798 and moved form Northeast Georgia to the Plains area after Indians were expelled in the 1830s. We set the date during his two hundredth anniversary year, but not having many current addresses, we issued a brief news bulletin that brought a deluge of responses. My computer records showed that most of them were not Wiley's descendants or even related to us, and we sent them polite notes of regret. The most delightful development was that many of our unknown relatives were located, including the entire family of Wiley's twelfth child, his youngest son, Sterling, who had run away and disappeared in Texas when he was fourteen years old.

We had planned to assemble in the auditorium of Plains High School but soon realized that we would need a much larger space. We arranged to seat our relatives in twelve groups in the basketball gymnasium of nearby Georgia Southwestern State University, and representatives of each family gave personal histories—some hilarious. Sterling served as a sheriff in Texas and came back to Georgia to woo and marry his wife, Mary. After she died in Texas, he returned to Georgia, married her sister, Loua, and returned to Texas. In his will, he directed

> *The most delightful development was that many of our unknown relatives were located.*

that he "be buried between the two, but be tilted a little toward Loua."

Almost nine hundred relatives were present at this reunion, and after two days of excited reminiscences, we assembled on a hillside and had a panoramic photograph made. Since then, I've entered in my computer file all the genealogical corrections and additions that are sent to me, and I share them with one of my newfound cousins, who happens to be a Mormon with access to that church's genealogical records. Perhaps some of our great-grandchildren will repeat the process in the year 2098, in the stadium of the Atlanta Braves. (*Sharing Good Times,* 98–99)

President Jimmy Carter surrounded by the First Presidency, receiving a gift in the Tabernacle on November 27, 1978

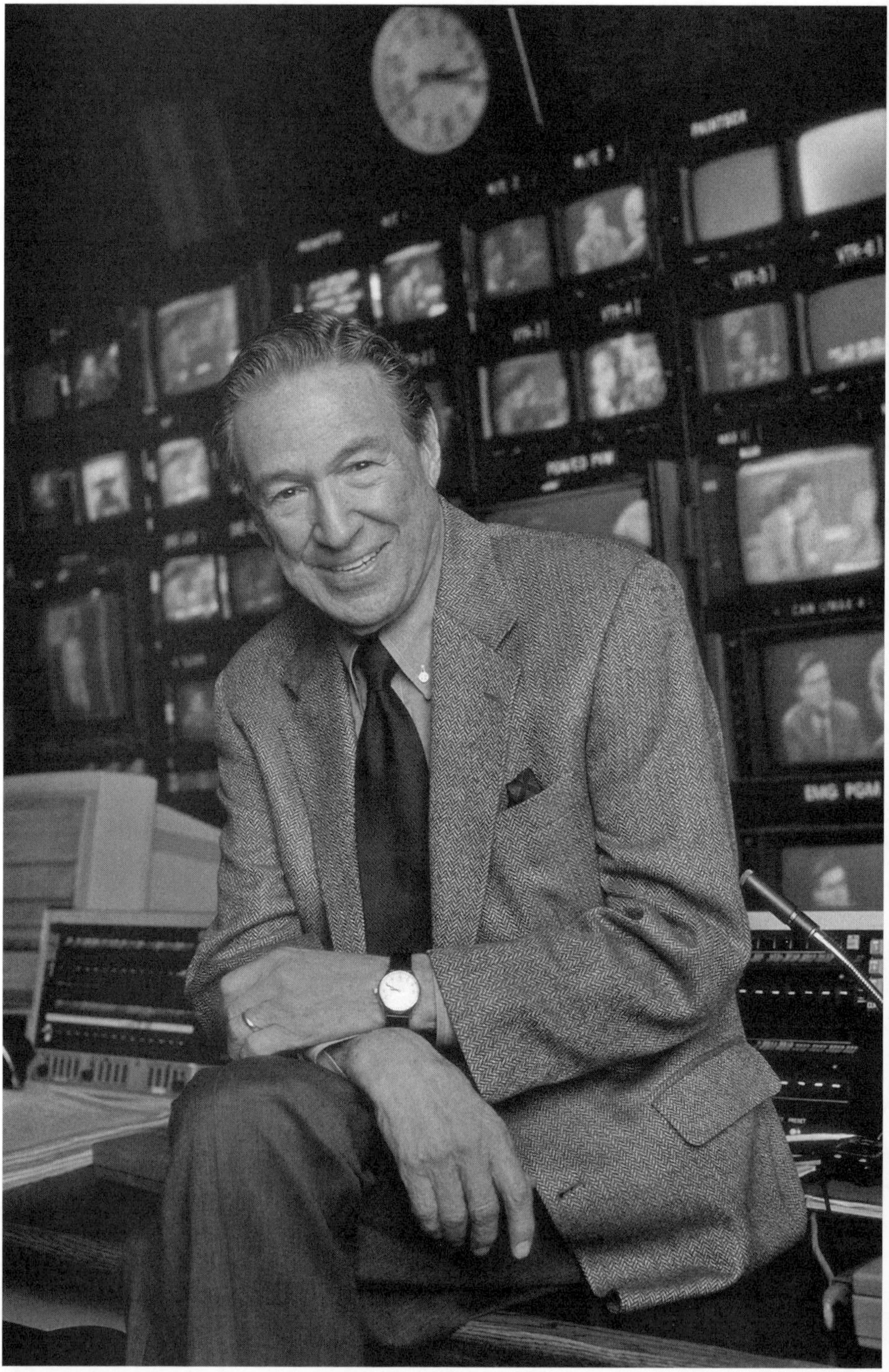

Mike Wallace

2005

CBS reporter Mike Wallace met President Gordon B. Hinckley when he conducted an interview with the prophet for 60 Minutes *in 1995. The two remained friends until Hinckley's death in 2008. In the following news article, Wallace—who was in town for Hinckley's 95th birthday celebration—told reporters about his friendship with the prophet and his opinions of the Church. He admired Hinckley's "courage and imagination," even though Wallace himself said he is not "a pious or religious fellow."*

> When you come out here and talk to people, you look in their eyes, they're so damned happy. Everyone looks so innocent. Maybe there's something we've been missing. ("Old Friend Mike Wallace in Town for Birthday Celebration," 22 July 2005)

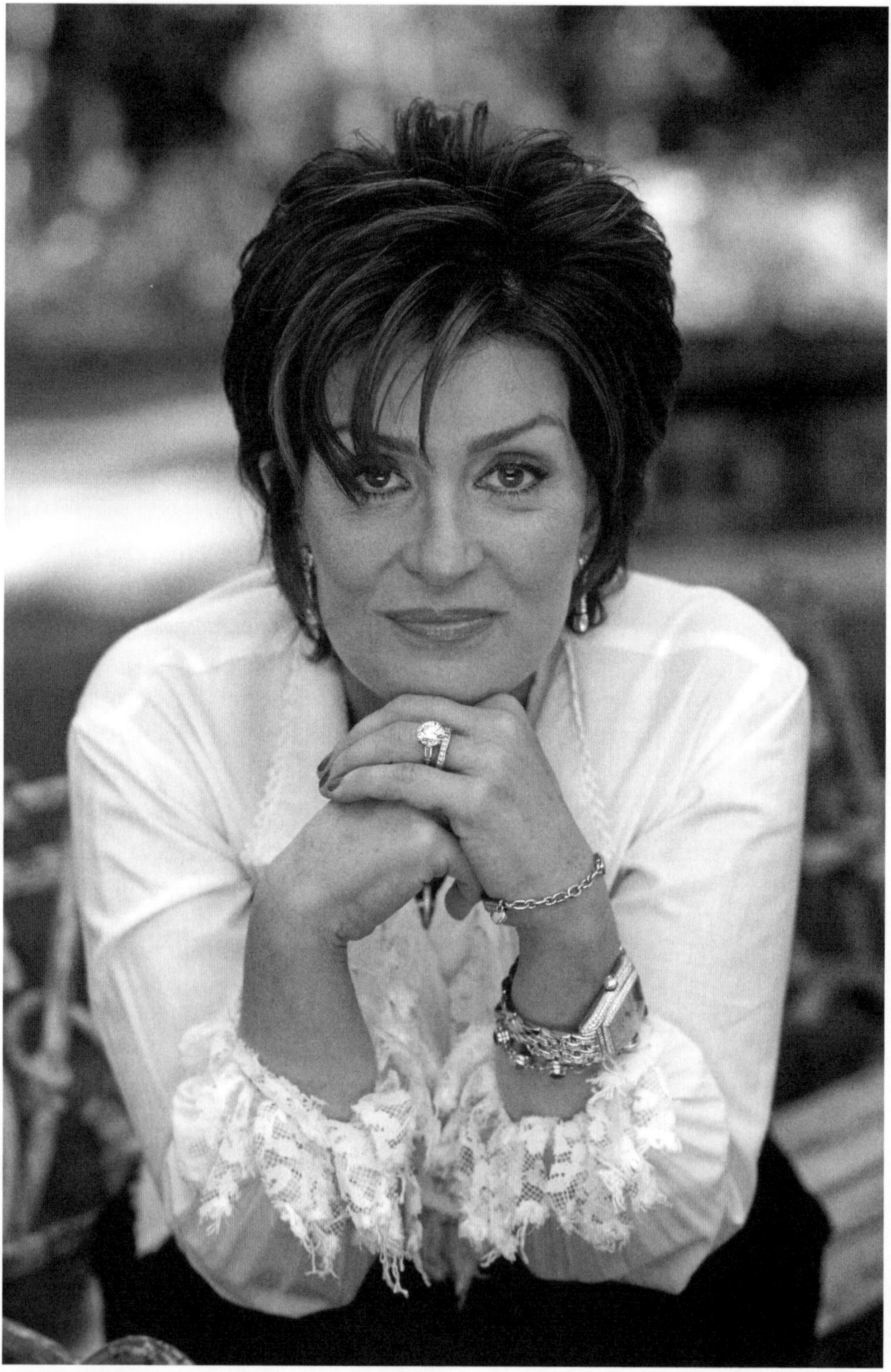

Sharon Osbourne

2005

*Sharon met rockstar "Ozzy" Osbourne when she was a teenager working for her father's management company. She later became not only Ozzy's career manager but also his wife, the mother of three children, president of her own international management company, and a talk-show host. She also started two record labels and her own charity. But perhaps she is best known for her idea to start a reality TV show—*The Osbournes. *The show won an Emmy for the best reality show and gave MTV high ratings. How does a woman who lives her life on national television find peace? At one point in her life, she looked to the temple.*

One of the first things I bought for the house was a big old-fashioned telescope, which I kept in the living-room area. And the first thing I did every night when I came home was go to the spyglass and look out across the city to the Mormon Temple on Santa Monica Boulevard. On top is a golden angel blowing a horn that glints at sunset. It was my ritual, a way of anchoring myself. And at night, with the city lit up, it was breathtaking. And I built a hot tub on the top terrace where you could sit and look out at it all glittering beneath you. (Sharon Osbourne, *Sharon Osbourne Extreme,* 86)

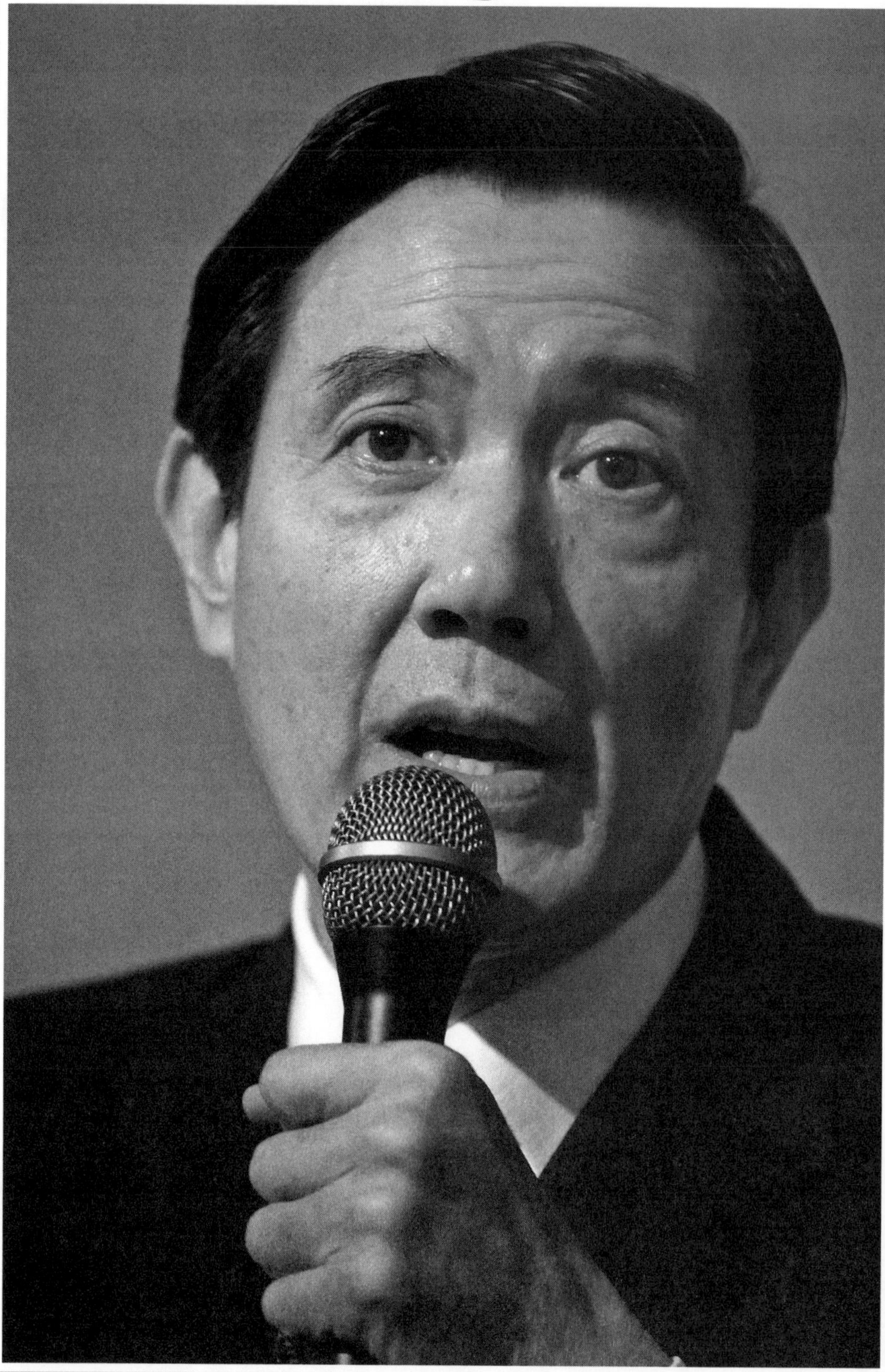

MA YING-JEOU
2008

Ma Ying-jeou, former mayor of Taipei and later president of Taiwan, was baptized a Catholic. While he didn't continue practicing the religion, he is still considered the first Catholic to be elected president in Taiwan. An article appeared in the Taipei Times, *quoting him regarding the contribution of Mormons missionaries to his country.*

> Their clean image elicits good feelings . . . [and they] promote energy conservation by using bicycles as their main mode of transport. (*Taipei Times,* 4)

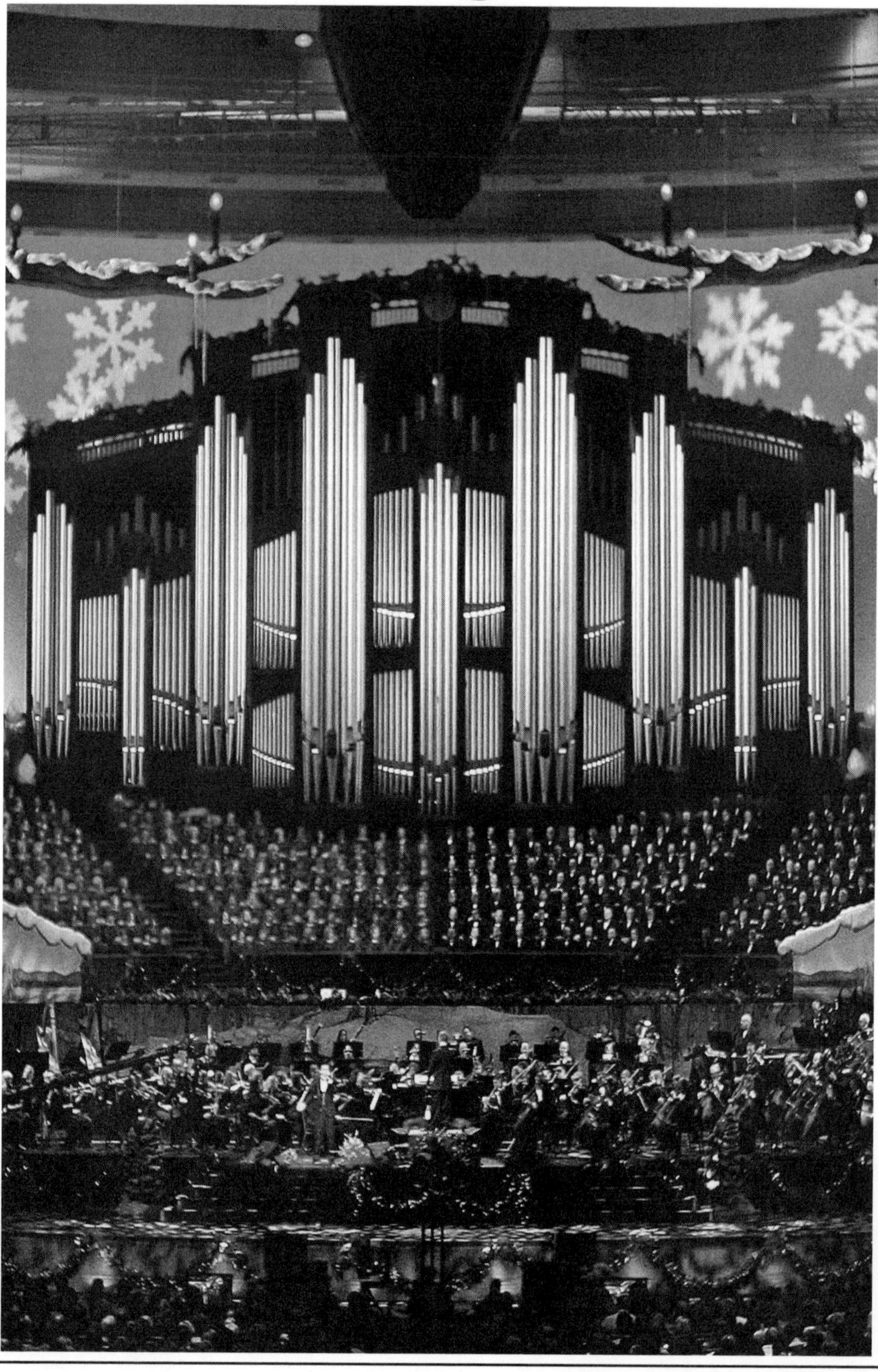

Mormon Tabernacle Choir Guests

Over the years, the Mormon Tabernacle Choir has performed with several talented guests, especially during their annual Christmas concerts. The following are comments from performers who enjoyed the opportunity to visit Salt Lake and perform with the choir.

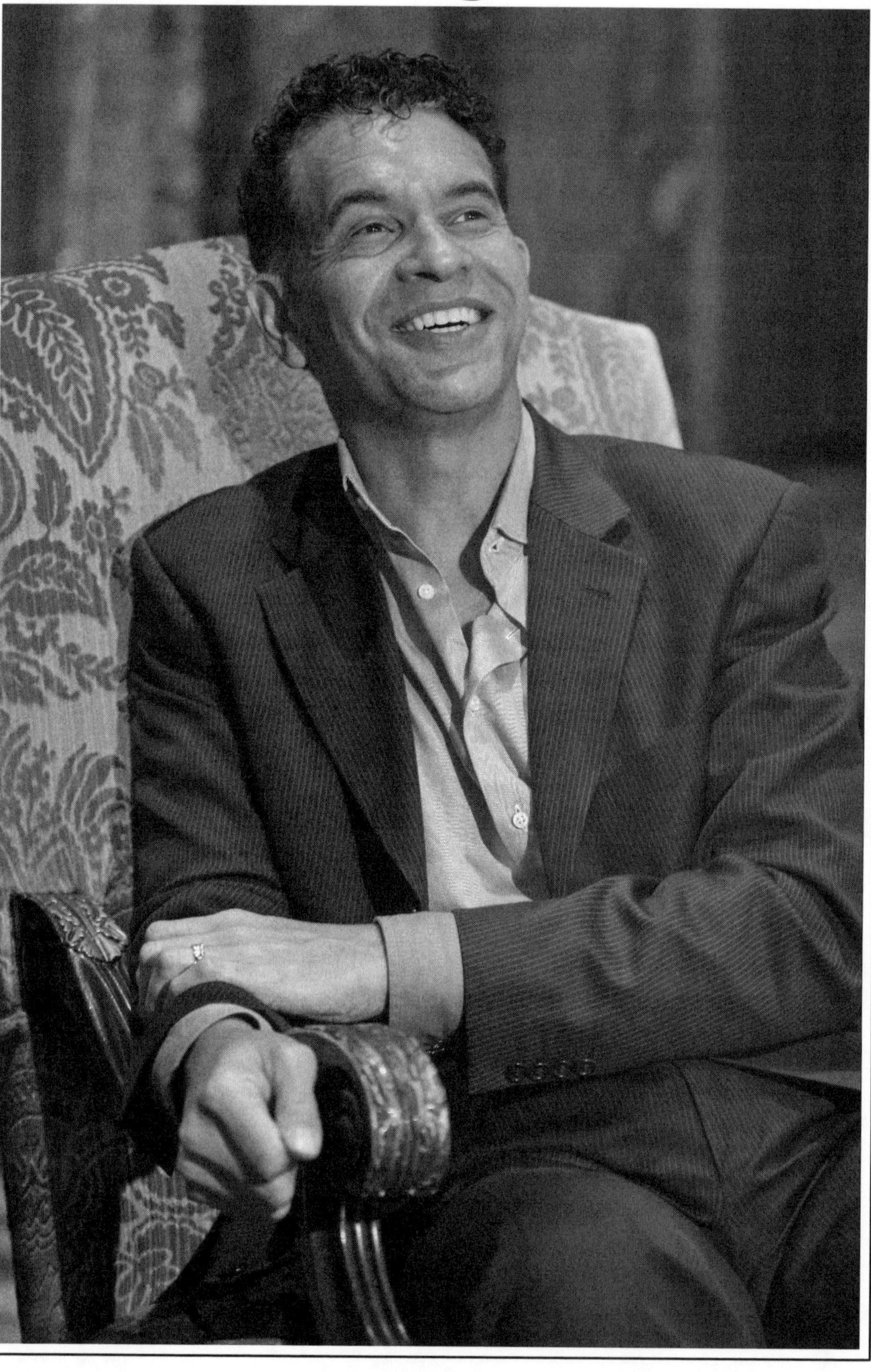

Brian Stokes Mitchell

2008

Brian Stokes Mitchell has enjoyed a rich and varied career on Broadway, in television, and in film, along with appearances in the great American concert halls, including work with John Williams, Alec Guinness, and James Earl Jones.

It's a remarkable experience working with the choir. I can't think of a better choir in the world to sing with. They are great artists individually and collectively. . . . There is a spiritual element here" that makes a huge difference. . . . It feels like coming home. (Reichel, Edward. "Guests enjoy working with Tabernacle Choir," *Deseret News*, 13 December 2008)

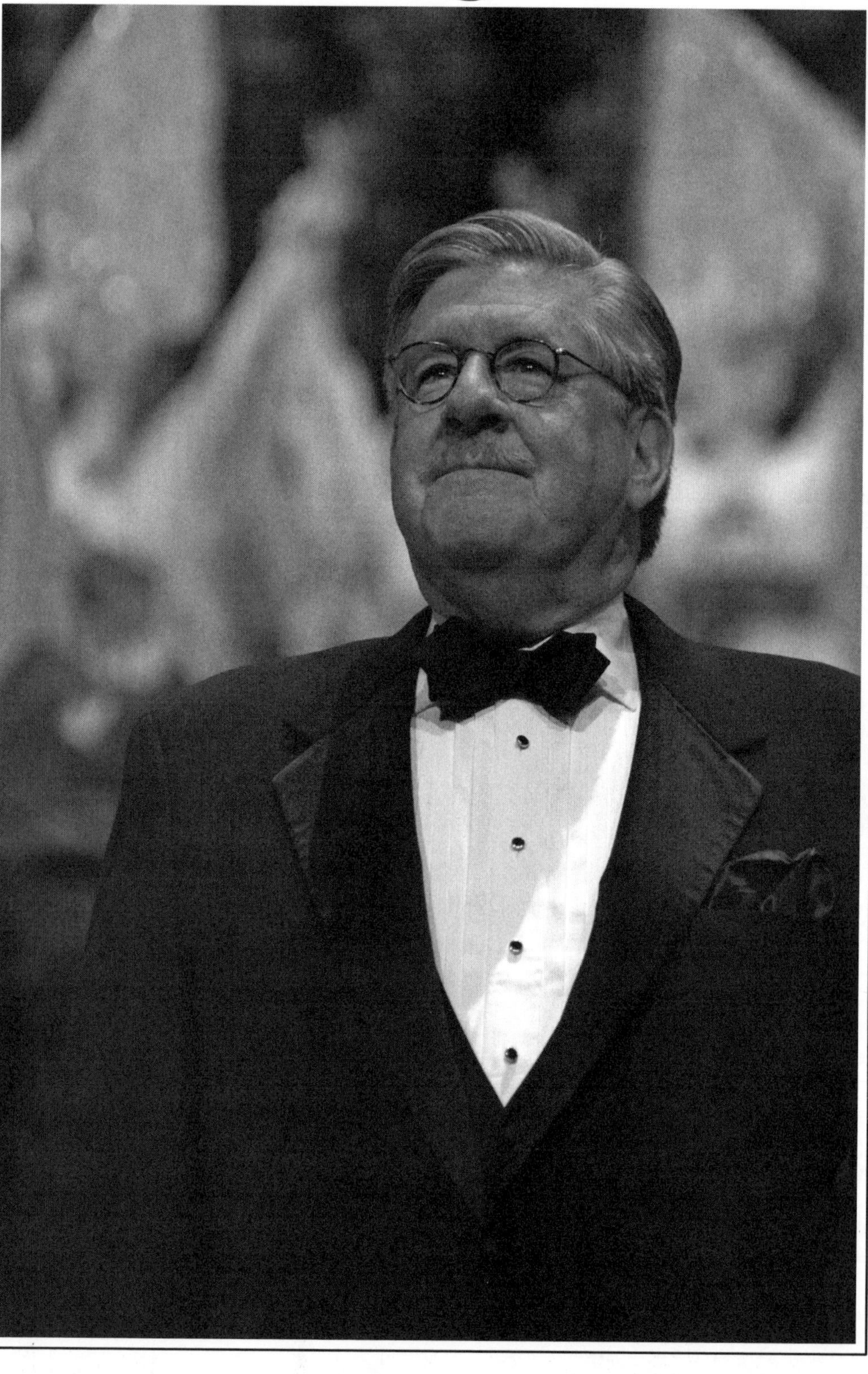

Edward Herrmann

2009

Tony-winning American stage and film actor Edward Herrmann used his Fulbright scholarship to study at London's Academy of Music and Dramatic Art. After several years of regional theater, his career led to movie and TV work, including Overboard, Gilmore Girls, Eleanor and Franklin, *and other works.*

I have been involved in theatrical and film productions for many years, some of them enormous, involving the biggest stars and directors and budgets in the business. But I must say that what happened in Salt Lake City surpassed my most extravagant expectations. The show involved the Mormon Tabernacle Choir, the Tabernacle Orchestra and bell ringers, scores of high school ringers and dancers, as well as the wonderful Brian Stokes Mitchell as soloist, and me, bringing up the rear, as guest reader.

More than 700 people were dashing around backstage, making entrances and exits, hitting marks and performing right on cue. If there was a minor kerfuffle, and I stress the word "minor," it was solved with a minimum of fuss and never happened again. The level of professional expertise was extraordinary.

And what truly amazed me was that everyone, from the greeters at the stage door to our indispensable guide and aide, Ron Gunnell, from the kids who rang the bells to the first chair fiddle players and musicians . . . all of them worked for nothing! And on top of that, everyone seemed delighted that I was there. "Thank you for coming to Salt Lake. We hope you like it here. We are so glad to have you." And, unless I have completely lost my sense of people, they meant it! I have never experienced anything

Narrator Edward Hermann and Brian Stokes Mitchell before a Christmas concert in the Conference Center in 2008

quite like the welcome I received during my stay in Utah this past Christmas.

So, I would like to thank the people of Utah, the folks in the choir and orchestra, the bell ringers and dancers, the people who helped manage and work the show, the technicians and designers and stage hands, and, of course, the folks who wrote and assembled the whole show. I had the time of my life. (Edward Herrmann, *Deseret News,* 29 January 2009)

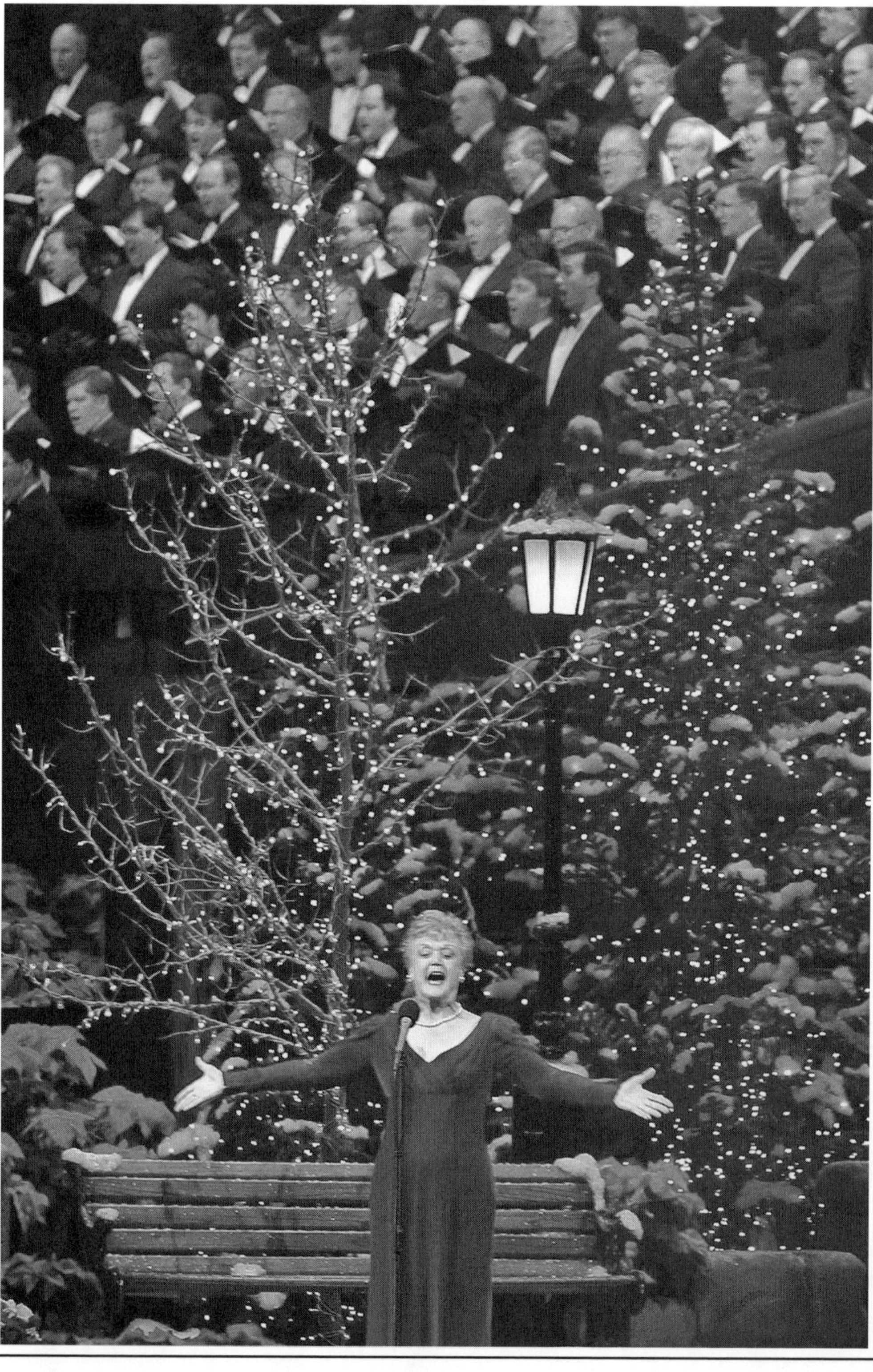

Angela Lansbury

2001

British actress Angela Lansbury is probably most well known for her role as Jessica Fletcher in Murder She Wrote. *She has also won multiple Tony Awards and was part of the award-winning Disney musical* Beauty and the Beast, *in which she costarred as Mrs. Potts.*

The spirit of this place is so evident. It is all enveloping. It's all around me. I feel buoyed up by it. This has been one of the things I felt very strongly about being here. I didn't realize that I was going to be hit by this extraordinary spirit. I haven't experienced this before. It's quite unique, people doing something for the love of it, not for the almighty [dollar], but just for the love of doing it, of joining together, expressing their sense of feelings about life and all of the qualities that are inherent to the Mormon Church. This is something that is all totally new to me. I had never been exposed to it, and I didn't understand what it was about. But I am really fascinated by it. (Gerry Avant, *Church News*)

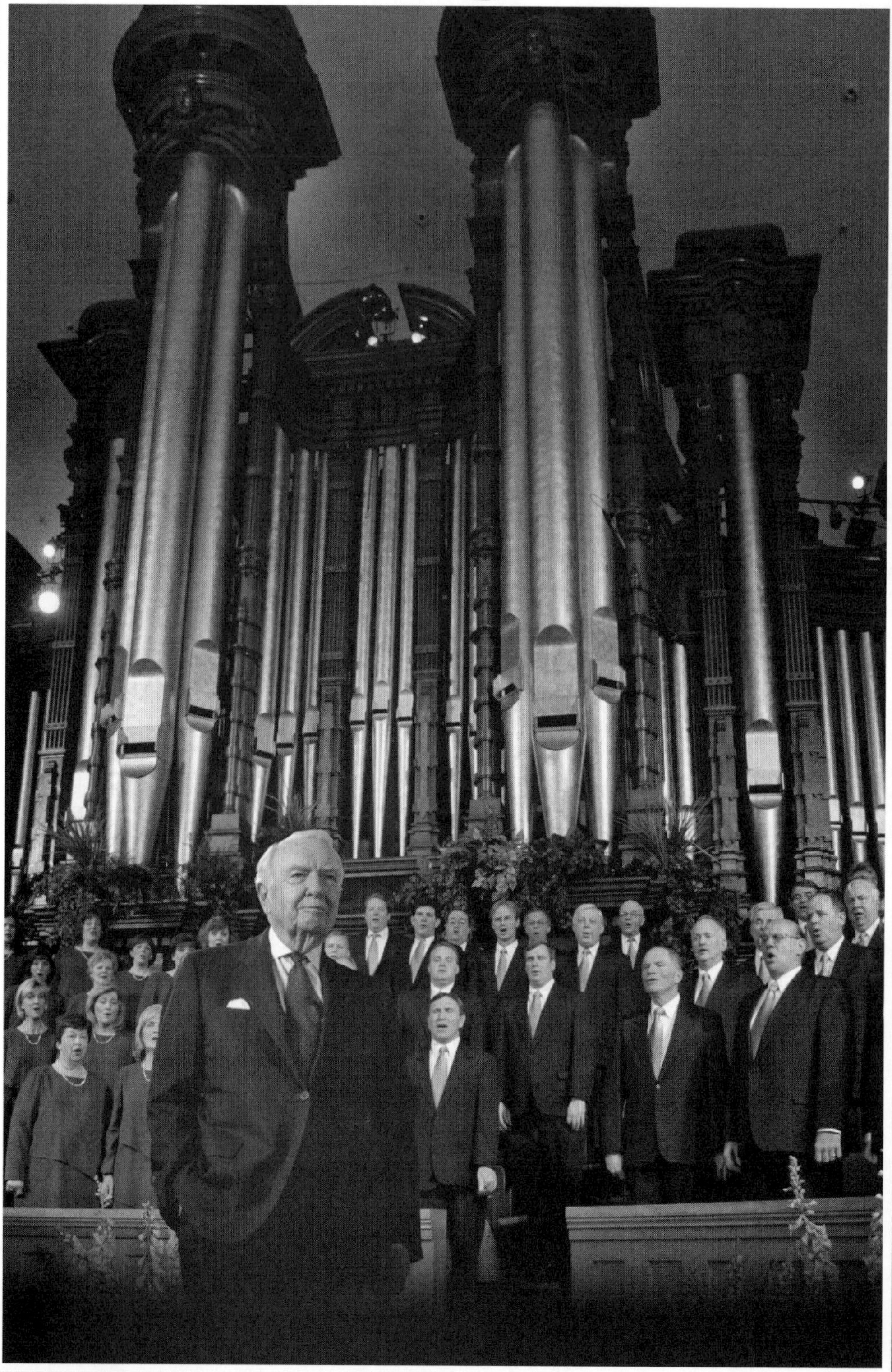

WALTER CRONKITE

2002

Known as one of the most trusted voices in America, Walter Cronkite anchored at CBS Evening News *for nearly two decades, covering such important events as the Kennedy assassination, the Vietnam War, the Cuban Missile Crisis, the moon landing, and Watergate.*

  I hope that somewhere, Mom and Dad are proud that little Walter is performing with the Mormon Tabernacle Choir.
  I have never been a religious person in the conventional sense, but I have felt nearer to my God the past couple of days than ever before. (Rob Cundick, *Meridian Magazine*)

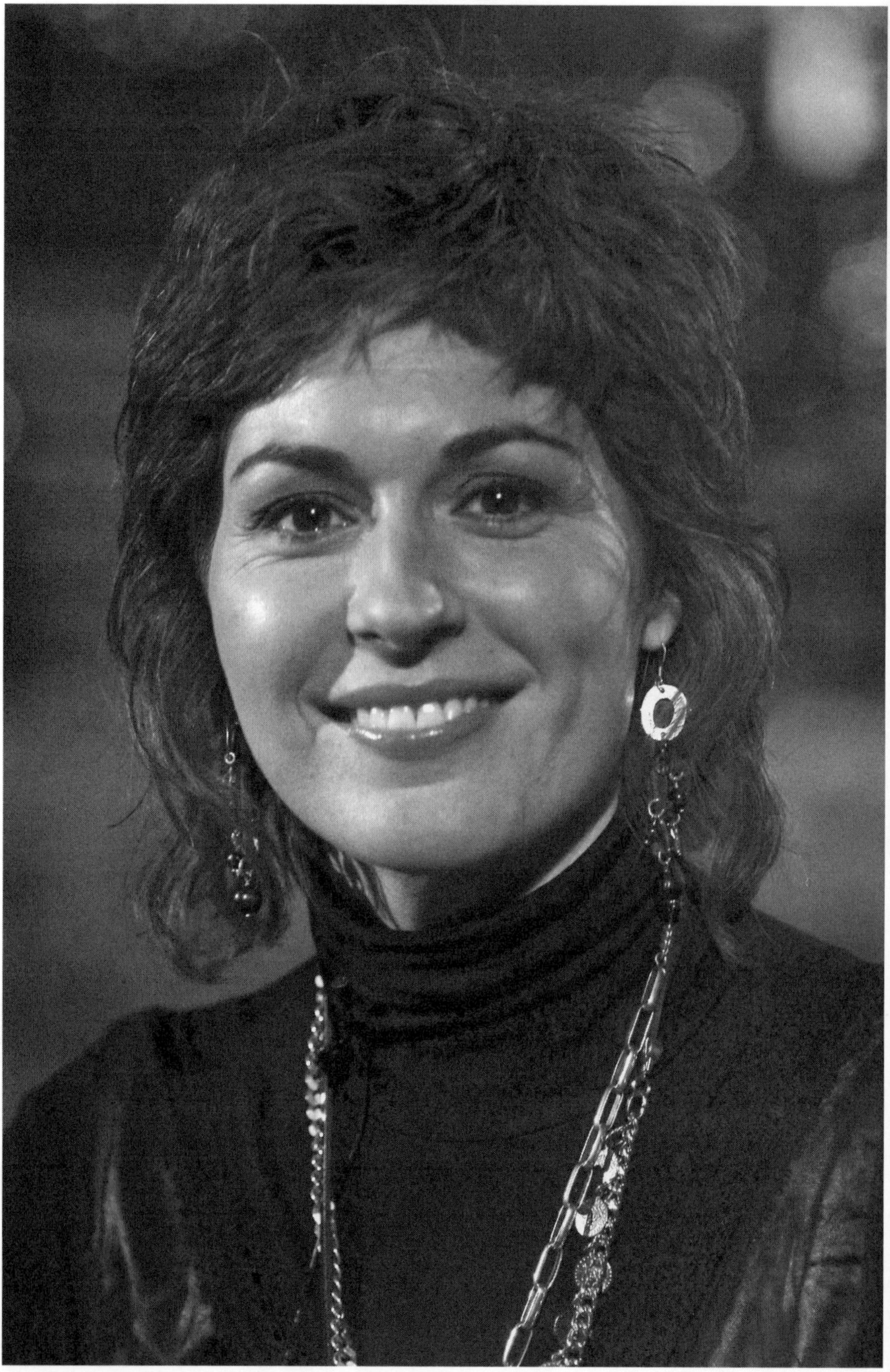

Sissel Kyrkjebo

2006

Sissel is well known for her multifaceted career in vocal performance, having performed with pop artists and symphonies, also having sung at Nobel Peace Prize concerts and Olympic Games. Her unique talent has brought fine music to the world for more than twenty years.

The [Conference Center] hall is something beyond imagination. [It is] enormous and amazing; and still, it's intimate. It's so strange—21,000, 22,000 people out there—and, I don't feel like I'm coming out there and I'm scared. It's not that I'm coming out in a stadium where it is cold. I feel like there is a presence—a presence of God in that room. For me it is like singing in a church. And it is so warm! . . .

There is so much to bring home—the joy of singing, the joy of sharing, the music. But most of all the love of the people—the love of the people that I've met. I really feel like I've been blessed—really—that I've been given this opportunity to come here, and meet everybody, and sing. I was so overwhelmed by this love. I will bring that with me and I will carry it. I will also try to learn something from it. It is important! (*Meridian Magazine* archive)

BIBLIOGRAPHY

ADAMS, CHARLES FRANCIS, and JOHN QUINCY
Winder, Michael K., *Presidents and Prophets: The Story of America's Presidents and the LDS Church,* American Fork, UT: Covenant Communications, 2007, 37–38.

ANTHONY, SUSAN B.
Anthony, Katharine Susan. *Susan B. Anthony: Her Personal History and Her Era,* Garden City, NY: Doubleday, 1954.

BARNUM, P. T.
Barnum, Phineas Taylor. *Struggles and Triumphs: or, Sixty Years' Recollections of P. T. Barnum, Including His Golden Rules for Money Making,* Buffalo, NY: The Courier Company, 1889.

BELLOW, SAUL
Bellow, Saul. *It All Adds Up: From the Dim Past to the Uncertain Future,* New York: Viking, 1994.

BURTON, SIR RICHARD
Burton, Sir Richard. *The City of the Saints, and Across the Rocky Mountains to California,* New York: Harper & Brothers, 1862; see also Burton, Sir Richard. *Wanderings in Three Continents,* ed. W. H. Wilkins., New York: Dodd, Mead & Co., 1901.

CARTER, JIMMY
Carter, Jimmy. *Sharing Good Times,* New York: Simon and Schuster, 2004.

CATHER, WILLA
Cather, Willa. *My Ántonia,* Boston: Houghton Mifflin, 1918.

CODY, WILLIAM FREDERICK
Cody, William F. *Life and Adventures of "Buffalo Bill,"* Chicago: John R. Stanton Co., 1917.

CUSTER, GENERAL GEORGE ARMSTRONG
Hirshson, Stanley P. *The Lion of the Lord: A Biography of Brigham Young,* New York: Alfred A. Knopf, 1969; see also Custer, George Armstrong. *Wild Life on the Plains and Horrors of Indian Warfare,* St. Louis, Mo., Sun Publishing Co., 1883.

DEMILLE, CECIL
DeMille, Cecil. BYU Commencement Address, 31 May 1957.

DICKENS, CHARLES
Dickens, Charles. *The Uncommercial Traveller,* Boston and New York: Houghton Mifflin Co., 1894.

DOYLE, SIR ARTHUR CONAN
Doyle, Sir Arthur Conan. *A Study in Scarlet,* New York: Harper & Brothers, 1904; Doyle, Sir Arthur Conan. *Our Second American Adventure, Boston:* Little, Brown & Co., 1924.
EMERSON, RALPH WALDO
Journals of Ralph Waldo Emerson, eds. Edward Waldo Emerson and Waldo Emerson Forbes, Boston: Houghton-Mifflin, 1913; see also Thayer, James B. *A Western Journey with Mr. Emerson,* Boston: Little, Brown & Co., 1884.
FORD, GERALD R.
Winder, Michael K., *Presidents and Prophets: The Story of America's Presidents and the LDS Church,* American Fork, UT: Covenant Communications, 2007.
GOLDEN, HARRY
Golden, Harry. "Only in America," *BYU Speeches of the Year, 1959–1960,* Provo, UT: BYU Extension Publications, 1959–1960.
GREELEY, HORACE
Greeley, Horace. *An Overland Journey, from New York to San Francisco, in the Summer of 1869,* New York: C. M. Saxton, Barker, and Co.; see also Greeley, Horace. Recollections of a Busy Life, New York: J. B. Ford & Co., 1868.
HARDY, LADY MARY DUFFUS
Hardy, Mary Duffus, Lady. *Through Cities and Prairie Lands: Sketches of an American Tour,* New York: R. Worthington, 1881.
HARDING, WARREN G.
Winder, Michael K., *Presidents and Prophets: The Story of America's Presidents and the LDS Church,* American Fork, UT: Covenant Communications, 2007.
HARRISON, BENJAMIN
Winder, Michael K., *Presidents and Prophets: The Story of America's Presidents and the LDS Church,* American Fork, UT: Covenant Communications, 2007.
HARVEY, PAUL
Faust, James E., "The Light in Their Eyes," *Ensign,* November 2005, 20.
HOOVER, HERBERT
Winder, Michael K., *Presidents and Prophets: The Story of America's Presidents and the LDS Church,* American Fork, UT: Covenant Communications, 2007.

JOHNSON, LYNDON B.
Winder, Michael K., *Presidents and Prophets: The Story of America's Presidents and the LDS Church,* American Fork, UT: Covenant Communications, 2007.

KANE, ELIZABETH
Kane, Elizabeth Wood. *Twelve Mormon Homes Visited in Succession on a Journey through Utah to Arizona,* Philadelphia: n.p., 1874.

KENNEDY, JOHN F.
Kennedy, John F. Speech given in the Mormon Tabernacle on 23 September 1960. John T. Woolley and Gerhard Peters, The American Presidency Project. Santa Barbara, CA: University of California, http://www.presidency.ucsb.edu/ws/?pid=74176.

Winder, Michael K., Presidents and Prophets: The Story of America's Presidents and the LDS Church, American Fork, UT: Covenant Communications, 2007.

LESLIE, MIRIAM FLORENCE
Leslie, Mrs. Frank. California: A Pleasure Trip from Gotham to the Golden Gate, New York: G. W. Carleton & Co., 1877.

LINCOLN, ABRAHAM
In Nibley, Preston. Brigham Young: The Man and His Work, Salt Lake City: Deseret News Press, 1936.

MORMON TABERNACLE CHOIR GUESTS
Avant, Gerry. "'I didn't realize that I was going to be hit by this extraordinary spirit,'" Church News, 15 December 2001.

Cundick, Robb. "Christmas with the Mormon Tabernacle Featuring Sissel," Meridian Magazine archive, http://www.meridianmagazine.com/music/071217sissel.html.

Cundick, Robb. "Silent Night, Holy Night: Walter Cronkite and the Mormon Tabernacle Choir," Meridian Magazine archive, http://www.meridianmagazine.com/music/021224silent.html.

Herrmann, Edward. "Utah Is a Source of Delight for Actor," Deseret News, January 29, 2009, http://findarticles.com/p/articles/mi_qn4188/is_20090129/ai_n31297222.

Reichel, Edward. "Guests enjoy working with Tabernacle Choir," Deseret News, 13 December 2008, http://www.deseretnews.com/article/705270092/Guests-enjoy-working-with-Tabernacle-Choir.html.

MUIR, JOHN
Muir, John. *Steep Trails,* ed. by William Frederick Badè, Boston and New York: Houghton Mifflin Company, 1918.

NIXON, RICHARD M.
Winder, Michael K., *Presidents and Prophets: The Story of America's Presidents and the LDS Church,* American Fork, UT: Covenant Communications, 2007.

OSBOURNE, SHARON
Osbourne, Sharon. Sharon Osbourne Extreme: My Autobiography, New York: Springboard Press, 2005.

PEALE, NORMAN VINCENT
Peale, Norman Vincent. "Why Positive Thinkers Get Positive Results," address given on 22 October 1963 in *BYU Speeches of the Year, 1963.* Salt Lake City: Deseret Book, 2011.

POLK, JAMES K.
Polk, James Knox. *The Diary of James K. Polk During His Presidency, 1845–1849,* 4 vols., ed. Milo Milton Quaife, Chicago: A. C. McClurg & Co., 1910.

PRICE, VINCENT
Price, Vincent. "The Enjoyment of Great Art," address given on 30 November 1959, in *BYU Miscellaneous Speeches,* 1959, Provo, UT: BYU Extension Publishers, 1959.

ROOSEVELT, FRANKLIN D.
Winder, Michael K. *Presidents and Prophets: The Story of America's Presidents and the LDS Church,* American Fork, UT: Covenant Communications, 2007.

ROOSEVELT, THEODORE
Improvement Era, vol. XIV, no. 3, Salt Lake City: General Board YMMIA, 1911.

THATCHER, MARGARET
Thatcher, Margaret. "The Moral Challenges for the Next Century," in *BYU Speeches,* 5 March 1996.

TOFFLER, ALVIN
Toffler, Alvin. *The Third Wave,* New York: William, Morrow and Co., 1980.

TRAPP, MARIA VON
Trapp, Maria Von. "The Real Story of Maria von Trapp," address given on 18 November 1965, in *BYU Speeches of the Year 1965,* Salt Lake City: Deseret Book, 2011.

TRUMAN, HARRY S
Winder, Michael K. *Presidents and Prophets: The Story of America's Presidents and the LDS Church,* American Fork, UT: Covenant Communications, 2007.

TWAIN, MARK
Twain, Mark. *Roughing It,* New York: Harper Brothers, 1913.

WALLACE, MIKE
Carole Mikita, "'Old Friend' Mike Wallace in Town for Birthday Celebration,'" 22 July 2005, as found at www.adherents.com/people/pw/Mike_Wallace.html.

WHITTIER, JOHN GREENLEAF
Whittier, John Greenleaf. *The Stranger in Lowell,* Boston: Waite, Peirce and Company. No. 1 Cornhill, 1845.

YING-JEOU, MA
"Ma lauds Mormon Church," *Taipei Times,* 16 July 2008, http://www.taipeitimes.com/News/taiwan/archives/2008/07/16/2003417620.

PHOTO CREDITS

Library of Congress: Courtesy of Library of Congress Prints and Photographic Division, Washington, DC.
Utah State Historical Society: Used by permission, Utah State Historical Society, all rights reserved.

Page vi Library of Congress
Page 2 Library of Congress
Page 3 Library of Congress
Page 4 Library of Congress
Page 7 Library of Congress
Page 10 Library of Congress
Page 14 Library of Congress
Page 17 Utah State Historical Society
Page 18 Library of Congress
Page 22 Library of Congress
Page 25 Library of Congress
Page 26 Library of Congress
Page 29 Library of Congress
Page 30 Library of Congress
Page 32 Library of Congress
Page 35 Courtesy of LDS Church Archives. Photographer: Charles Roscoe Savage, ca. 1861–64
Page 36 Library of Congress
Page 39 Utah State Historical Society
Page 40 Library of Congress
Page 44 Library of Congress
Page 48 Library of Congress
Page 50 Library of Congress
Page 52 Library of Congress
Page 54 Library of Congress
Page 60 Library of Congress
Page 69 Library of Congress
Page 72 Library of Congress
Page 74 Library of Congress
Page 76 Library of Congress
Page 78 Library of Congress
Page 80 Utah State Historical Society
Page 93 Library of Congress
Page 96 American Editor and Publisher Miriam Florence Leslie © CORBIS, ca. 1870s
Page 98 Deseret News

Page 106 Library of Congress
Page 108 Library of Congress
Page 120 Library of Congress
Page 124 Library of Congress
Page 125 Library of Congress
Page 126 Library of Congress
Page 128 Library of Congress
Page 130 Universtiy of Utah Marriott Library Special Collections.
Page 132 Courtesy of Special Collections Department, J. Willard Marriott Library University of Utah. Used by permission
Page 134 Courtesy of the Nebraska State Historical Society, Willa Cather Pioneer Memorial Collection.
Page 136 Library of Congress
Page 138 Library of Congress
Page 140 Library of Congress
Page 146 Library of Congress
Page 148 Library of Congress
Page 150 Library of Congress
Page 152 Library of Congress
Page 156 Library of Congress
Page 159 Deseret News
Page 160 Deseret News
Page 164 Deseret News
Page 166 Library of Congress
Page 169 Deseret News
Page 170 Deseret News
Page 173 Deseret News
Page 174 Deseret News
Page 176 Deseret News
Page 178 Library of Congress
Page 180 Lyndon B. Johnson LBJ Library Photo by: Yoichi R. Okamoto, Januar 1969. Courtesy of Wikimedia commons; for more information, visit www.commons.wikimedia.org.
Page 182 Singer Maria Augusta Trapp © Bettmann/CORBIS, ca. 1950s.
Page 184 Paul Harvey Broadcasting © Bettmann/CORBIS, ca. August 31, 1980
Page 186 Both Deseret News
Page 187 Deseret News
Page 188 Library of Congress
Page 190 both Deseret News
Page 192 Top: Ford, Kimball, and Primary kids. Courtesy of LDS Church Archives, Salt Lake City, Utah.
Bottom: Ford and Pres. Kimball. Courtesy of LDS Church Archives, Salt Lake City, Utah.
Page 198 Saul Bellow © Nancy Crampton, www.nancycrampton.com.
Page 202 Library of Congress
Page 204 Deseret News
Page 206 Deseret News
Page 208 Deseret News
Page 210 Sharon Osbourne © Neal Preston/CORBIS, ca. 2002
Page 212 Ma Ying-jeou speaks © NICKY LOH/Reuters/Corbis, April 27, 2010.
Page 214 Deseret News
Page 216 Deseret News
Page 218 Deseret News
Page 219 Deseret News
Page 221 Deseret News
Page 223 Deseret News

Rick Walton is the author of more than eighty books, most of them for children and young readers. Among some of his most notable books are his bunny series with HarperCollins, *Pig Pigger Piggest,* and *The Remarkable Friendship of Mr. Cat and Mr. Rat.* He has worked with many national and regional publishers. One of his career-long pursuits has also been to teach and train up-and-coming writers and artists, part of which he does by teaching publishing classes at Brigham Young University and at various conferences. He lives in Provo, Utah, with his family.